The Last Corner of Arabia

The Last Corner of Arabia

Michael Darlow and Richard Fawkes

Edited by
Naim Attallah

Photographs by
Robin Constable and Peter Middleton

NAMARA PUBLICATIONS | QUARTET BOOKS   LONDON

Young boy on the steps of the Mosque, Sur.

First published in 1976 by
Namara Publications Limited
and Quartet Books Limited
27 Goodge Street, London W1P 1FD

Copyright © 1976
by Namara Publications Limited

Design by Mike Jarvis

ISBN 0 704 32109 2

Printed in Great Britain by
Gavin Martin Limited, Wallington, Surrey
and Anchor Press Limited of Tiptree, Essex
and bound by William Brendon & Son Limited
of Tiptree, Essex

Koranic School, Rostaq.

For the people of Oman

Boys swimming, Muttrah.

Contents

Guard at Rostaq Fort, under a portrait of the Sultan.

Preface

In the eastern corner of Arabia, astride the Tropic of Cancer, lies the Sultanate of Oman. It covers an area of some 100,000 square miles; its western borders disappear into the vast sand oceans of the Rub al Khali, the Empty Quarter of Saudi Arabia, and to the east 1,000 miles of coast are washed by the waters of the Gulf of Oman and the Indian Ocean.

Before 1970, few outsiders had visited Oman. Sultan Said bin Taimur ruled his country as a medieval society, deliberately isolating it from the outside world and preserving a way of life that had not changed for centuries. When his son Qaboos became Sultan in July 1970, Oman embarked on a development programme faster than any other country has ever seen.

We were invited to make a film about Oman five years after the takeover. This book springs from our experience there. It does not attempt to be a history, or a guide book; many places are not mentioned at all. It is a personal impression of a strange, remote and little-known kingdom.

The backbone of Oman is the Hajar mountain range, running north to south of the country from the tip of the Musandum peninsula to Ras al Hadd, the easternmost corner of Arabia. Musandum commands the straits through which the oil tankers of the Gulf pass – on average, one every ten minutes – and is cut off from the rest of Oman by a strip of territory belonging to the United Arab Emirates.

Further south, the mountains rise from 5,000 to 10,000 feet at their highest point in the Jebal Akhdar, a virtually inaccessible plateau in the centre of a range that is never more than forty-five miles wide. Between the mountains and the sea, north-west of the capital, Muscat, is the Batinah Coast, a 200-mile stretch of unbroken sand, fringed with palms. To the west of the Hajar, stretching out to the sweeping dunes of the Empty Quarter, are high gravel plains, about 3,000 feet above sea level.

Far away to the south, across hundreds of miles of desert, lies the province of Dhofar, where the Sultanate borders the People's Democratic Republic of Yemen. Dhofar resembles the north in that, behind a coastal plain and mountains, arid wastes stretch away towards Saudi Arabia; but it is touched by the monsoon and so has a tropical climate.

Our film crew consisted of cameraman Peter Middleton, his assistant Bob McShane, sound recordist John Hayes, electrician John Rogers, and Steve Thomas, an American Peace Corps worker who was loaned to us by the Ministry of Information, to whom we were very grateful. Steve's rudimentary knowledge of Arabic, and his love of Oman, were to prove useful on many occasions. We were also joined for some time by Robin Constable, whose photographs are featured in this book.

During our stay in Oman we all made many friends who gave us invaluable help; especially His Excellency Qais Zawawi, Colonel Malcolm Dennison, Major Salim Ghazali and Mr Andy Reid-Anderson.

Finally we must thank John Asprey for his initial help, Michael Deakin, co-author of *The Arab Experience*, who read the proofs, and Naim Attallah, executive producer of the film, whose tireless enthusiasm for both film and book has proved invaluable.

The following two books were found to be helpful whilst researching this book: *Muscat and Oman: the end of an Era* by Ian Skeet, published by Faber & Faber; *Arabian Assignment* by David Smiley, published by Leo Cooper.

MICHAEL DARLOW AND RICHARD FAWKES

Oman-Where?

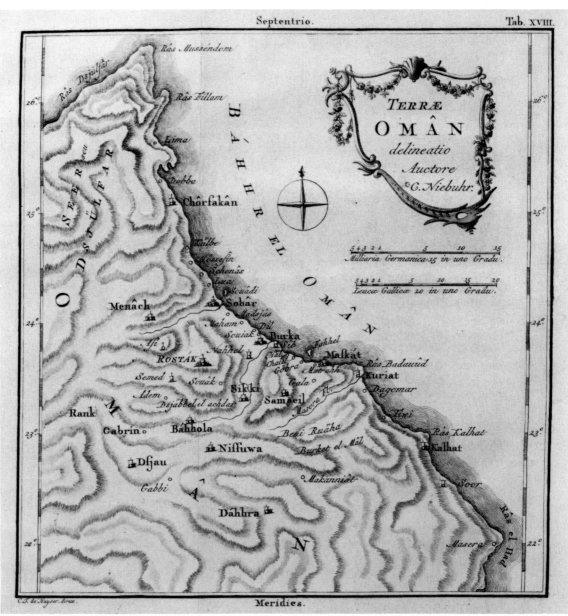

A map of the Gulf and Oman
from 'Descriptions of Arabia',
by Carsten Niebuhr, c. 1774.

'The Sultan of Oman wants a film made.' That was the first that I heard. To me, in a television executive's office in London, with grey January rain falling outside, it sounded mysterious and romantic. It was arranged that I would meet a man who was in contact with the Sultan. I went home to discover what I could about Oman. This was not very much; everything was clearly destined to be a fresh experience.

I could not even find out what equipment would be needed. The various contacts who were to brief me simply said, 'Don't worry; everything will be provided by the Sultan.' I confess that I was uneasy, especially when I read how carefully the great British explorer Wilfred Thesiger had prepared for his journey into Oman. On top of this, Oman's relaxed sense of time seemed to have spread to London. Again and again I was told that I would be going 'next week'. Everything seemed to depend on meeting a certain Colonel Landon, the Sultan's equerry and a legendary figure. Tim Landon had shared a room at Sandhurst with Qaboos, and had been at his side ever since; after the Sultan, he was one of the most influential men in the country, I was told. Then, one Saturday at the beginning of March, I was summoned to an address in Mayfair. I was let in by a white-robed servant, in silence, and shown to a beautifully furnished sitting-room. Eventually Landon appeared. He was bronzed, boyish, open-shirted. He spoke very quietly. Later I noticed that all the British who had served in Oman for any length of time spoke quietly -- it seemed to be an effect that the country had on them.

Landon told me that I was to leave in a week's time. The film should take two weeks to re-search and organize, followed by three weeks of shooting. We would be finished by mid-April, before the weather got too dangerously hot. I was to fly direct to Muscat, the capital, where I would be met. There, an NOC – a 'No Objections Certificate' – would be waiting for me.

'And what about equipment?' I asked. 'Shall I take anything special?' Landon looked blank.

'Well,' I continued tentatively, not wishing to imply that I doubted the Sultan's hospitality, 'do I need a sleeping bag?'

'Good Lord, yes,' he said, 'and a camp bed. You need something to keep you off the ground so that the scorpions don't get in with you.' He must have seen the look of surprise on my face, because he added, 'When I leave the capital I have to sleep under any tree I can find, so there's no chance that you will be provided with a bed for the night. I'll give you another tip. When you wake up in the morning always shake your shoes out, because you'll find the scorpions and the camel spiders like sleeping in them.'

A week later, I set off. It takes eleven hours from London to Muscat, so when I arrived at one o'clock in the morning I was perhaps not at my brightest. It was March, but already a wall of humid heat seemed to push you back as you stepped out of the aircraft. In the modern terminal building, our small, confused crowd of passengers was watched over by amiable, well-armed Omani policemen, their uniforms clearly modelled on those of British colonial police forces: light khaki drill, blue peaked cap with chequered band. An official came round calling out names and handing out NOCs. My name was not on his list. I went into his office and we checked through all his lists – businessmen, soldiers, health experts, United Nations officials from all round the globe – but my name was not among them. I explained that I had come to see about making a film with the approval of the Sultan himself, and that Colonel Landon had promised that a Foreign Office official would meet me with a car to take me to the Al Falaj Hotel. Now it was all too apparent that something had gone wrong, and there was quite plainly nobody to meet me. By two o'clock the other passengers had all got through immigration and customs, and they were preparing to shut the airport for the night. Then my friendly official had a bright idea. He went to check with one of the policemen manning the immigration cubicles whether my name might be on some special list of his. It was.

Outside I was besieged by half a dozen taxi drivers all dressed in white gowns called *dish-dashas* and all driving Japanese cars. I chose one and climbed in beside the driver. I turned to him and said, 'The Al Falaj Hotel.' It was then that I realized that the driver had only one eye.

Leaving the bright lights of the airport, we were enveloped in hot black night. The air coming through the open car windows carried the incessant noise of cicadas. It was hot and clammy; sweat began to roll off me in layers. In the distance there was the thin outline of mountains; closer to the car, headlights picked out stunted bushes on either side of the road. It was a bizarre situation. I was 4,000 miles from home, driving along an unmarked road in a country supposedly given to unrest with a one-eyed driver with whom I couldn't exchange more than two words. At that moment torches started to flash on the road in front of us. The car came to a halt and a policeman put his head through the window. It was a police check, the first of many I

ran into on roads all over Oman. The policeman and my driver exchanged a few pleasantries, and we drove on.

After about half an hour we drew up outside a modern European-style hotel – the Al Falaj. The man behind the desk said they had no rooms.

'But one has been booked for me by the Palace.'

The man consulted his lists. 'No,' he said, 'no one of your name here. Perhaps you are in the Annexe.'

'Where's that?' I asked, presuming it must be through the back.

'Oh, it's not here,' he said, 'you'll have to go in a taxi.'

We set off again round half-finished roundabouts, down roads flanked with scaffolding, for all the world like a gigantic building site. Ten minutes later we bumped and crawled in a cloud of dust up a potholed track, coming to a halt outside a low prefabricated concrete building – the Annexe. I paid off the driver and was soon thankfully falling into bed in an uncarpeted concrete cubicle, sparsely furnished with a table, chair and wardrobe.

Next morning, I was awoken by an Indian room boy who had come to make the bed. It was eight o'clock, the sun was streaming through the windows, and the temperature was already well into the nineties. I made my way downstairs where I asked to use the telephone. I had been given some contact numbers, and I thought I should announce my arrival. After the previous night's mishap I thought people might be worried about where I was. 'We don't have a telephone,' said the boy behind the desk, 'you have to go to the main hotel for that.'

'That's miles away,' I said.

THE WATERCOLOURS SHOWN ON THIS AND
THE FOLLOWING PAGE ARE REPRODUCED BY KIND
PERMISSION OF THE SEAWRIGHT COLLECTION.

THE FORTS OF JEHALI AND MERANI, MUSCAT.
ENGRAVING BY J. C. ARMITAGE, FROM THE DRAWING BY W. DANIELL, R.A. 1836.

MUSCAT HARBOUR FROM THE FISHER-MEN'S ROCK. R. TEMPLE. 1813

MUSCAT FROM THE HARBOUR. R. TEMPLE. 1813

A VIEW OF THE MUTRA FROM THE EAST. R. TEMPLE. 1813

View of Muscat.

He shrugged his shoulders and smiled. 'There must be one nearer than that.'

'Maybe,' he said, pointing out of the door, 'maybe over there.'

Across the track from the front door of the hotel stood a compound containing dilapidated sheds and workshops, plus two or three battered dust-covered lorries. A faded notice proclaimed, in English and Arabic, 'FALCON WORKS'. I climbed through the loose strands of rusting barbed wire that served as a fence. There seemed to be no one around. After I had peered into various sheds, opening doors on to long-silent and nameless pieces of machinery, an Omani called to me from across the yard. I went over and we shook hands. Travelling abroad has turned me into a great hand-shaker, but Oman has every other country beaten for frequency and enthusiasm. With dumb-show and much repetition of the word 'telephone', I managed to explain to the man what I wanted. He took me into an office and from behind a pile of ledgers produced a brand-new telephone.

As my flight had been to Muscat, I assumed that I was now in Muscat. I had four contact numbers and dialled them one after the other. In each case I got an Arabic voice that didn't understand what I was going on about. However, during the fourth call I heard a click and for a few seconds a voice speaking in English. I interrupted the conversation. 'Excuse me,' I said, hoping that they could hear me, 'but if you were in the Al Falaj Hotel Annexe what would you dial for Muscat?'

'Ah,' said the voice, 'you're not in Muscat at all, you're in Ruwi. For Muscat you must dial 8 and for Muttrah you must dial 6.'

I tried my contacts again. First one, no reply; next Tim Landon – a secretary told me he was out of town, but where could he call me back? As the phone I was using didn't have a number on it and the hotel didn't have a phone at all, I couldn't give her much help. It was four weeks before I met Landon again. Next the Foreign Minister's personal assistant – a recorded message machine which also asked for a number where he could call me back. Finally, I tried Colonel Malcolm Dennison, Security Adviser to the Sultan, one of the people I had met fleetingly in London. 'Ah,' he said, 'so you've got here. Well, I should rest up for a bit if I were you, I don't think there's much we can do until next week.' I explained to him that as I had been advised that it would be too hot to film after the end of April, I needed to get on with my research quickly. He must have detected the note of desperation in my voice, because he agreed to come round that evening and try and sort something out. In fact, Malcolm Dennison was to prove one of my greatest allies in Oman. Without him our film would never have been made.

It was still only ten o'clock, and I thought it would be spineless to waste the rest of the day until Dennison came to see me. So I thanked the man for letting me use his telephone – he refused to take any money – and walked up the dust track leading away from the hotel. There I came to a main road jammed with hooting lorries and taxis: Ruwi High Street. The crowded strip of tarmac was lined with rapidly constructed frontages, windows bulging with an incredible assortment of goods: Indian sweetmeats and Japanese tape-recorders, Coca-Cola and hurricane lamps. It was thronged with strolling, vociferous people, Indians, Pakistanis, Baluchis and Omanis. There were no women, except for a few sari-clad Indians. The men were dressed in a variety of clothes: jeans with Western shirts, or traditional Omani *dishdashas*, the straight white gowns which go down to the feet, while, on the head, they wore a cloth wrapped round like a loose turban, or, sometimes, a little embroidered skull-cap. Many of the men carried old rifles, while others carried small goat sticks. Round their waists, many had silver and gold embroidered belts, sometimes studded with ammunition, and at the front a great curved dagger in a richly ornamented sheath – the traditional Omani *khunjar* which is given to every boy when he reaches maturity. I had hardly arrived in the street before a taxi pulled up and the driver opened the door and beckoned me to get inside. Thinking this would be a good way to explore, I clambered in and said, 'Muscat'. I repeated it a number of times as clearly as I could. Off we went down the street, stopping every so often to take on more passengers. Eventually, we wound up in the biggest taxi park I have ever seen. Literally hundreds of brightly coloured Japanese cars, all with drivers touting for business on a single open space. Round it were shops, whose construction might be described as fading British Imperial. Beyond the shops, bare, brown rock rose to a height of perhaps 300 or 400 feet and reflected

Traditional house, Muttrah.

back the heat of the sun. Half-hidden through a gap I could make out the tower of a fort. This, I concluded, remembering descriptions and photographs, must be Muscat. I walked towards the fort, assuming that I would find the sea. Soon I was picking my way down narrow alleys where merchants peered out of shady doorways. After walking for fifteen minutes, I was in danger of getting lost and there was no sign of the sea. I retraced my steps while I could still remember the way back to the car park. It wasn't until the next day, when Malcolm Dennison showed me around, that I realized that I hadn't been in Muscat at all but in Muttrah, the old commercial centre of Oman.

Meeting an intelligence officer feels rather like meeting a psychiatrist. You feel that you are being assessed, that conclusions are being drawn from the words you use and the way you use them. Apart from one brief glimpse of Malcolm Dennison in London, I had known nothing about him except that he was ex-RAF, a very highly thought of intelligence officer, reputed to know Oman better than anyone else alive; that he had been wounded more than once during his twenty years of service with the Sultans of Oman; and that an insurgent land-mine had once blown up his Land Rover. As he came into my concrete cubicle in the Annexe that evening, I noticed that he walked with a slight limp. He was a round-faced, bronzed man of medium height and stocky build. The other thing one noticed at once was his quiet voice, with a hint of a Highland accent; his eyes were friendly, but somehow far-seeing, such as you see in men who have spent a lot of time alone and in the open.

Malcolm Dennison is a man who takes a long time to get to know. That first evening,

sitting on the bed and drinking the whisky I had brought from London, I got no more than an impression of a pleasant, correct British officer of the old school. His strongest characteristic seemed to be total reserve; I couldn't tell whether that was the professional equipment of the intelligence officer or a cover for shyness. In his book *Arabian Assignment*, Colonel David Smiley describes Malcolm Dennison as he knew him in the 1950s: 'a quiet young man of gentle but persuasive charm and tireless persistence, who spoke fluent Arabic, he would exercise his talents, without violence but with the most gratifying results, on suspected enemy agents'. Dennison stayed for only half an hour, but before he left he had agreed to show me around the country and promised that he would return next morning to 'try to get you into one or two of the ministries'.

Duly, at half-past seven next morning, Malcolm Dennison appeared at the hotel. Government offices in Oman are open from eight until one; after that it is too hot to work. First we drove down into Muscat – six or seven miles.

The first view of Muscat is as spectacular as everyone says it is. As you approach over the brow of a hill, the little town is laid out before you, squeezed between towering rocks, dominated by ancient fortresses on either side, and facing the shimmering Indian Ocean. We wound our way down the old road in a queue of cars and trucks, picking our way among bright-robed Baluchi women, carrying water-jars on their heads, and agile, foraging goats. I suppose I had expected to see camels, but the animal that dominates Oman is the goat.

We drew up outside the Foreign Ministry, a new office block on the waterfront. It was the

Foreign Minister who was the official sponsor of my visit. The two men on the door knew Malcolm Dennison, and we were told to go straight up to the Minister's office. The Minister wasn't in, and his secretary didn't know when he would be there. Dennison deposited me in a chair in the under-secretary's office. 'You may have to sit there some time,' he said, 'but don't move until you've seen the Minister.' With that he left me.

It is always important when setting up a television programme to go and be polite to the authorities first. But in Oman this sort of thing takes on a character quite different from anything we know in the West. It is at the same time a long-drawn-out ritual and a totally casual and un-scheduled social affair. Nobody is surprised if you come at a completely different time from the one arranged or without any appointment at all. Indeed, one of the things that international salesmen find hardest to adjust to in Oman is the local sense of time. And so, while no one in the office seemed really to expect me, they equally did not seem at all perturbed when I appeared and sat there. Richard Fawkes and I both found later that we could walk into senior government officials' offices and sit down and wait. People would bring us coffee and orange juice, but never inquired what we wanted unless we pressed the matter ourselves. They seemed satisfied that we had come in an affable way to spend a little time sitting with them as friends.

On this occasion I sat for almost two hours in the office, and during that time I made up my mind that if I got to see the Minister I would make it more than a courtesy visit. Qais Zawawi has the reputation for being the most decisive man in the country. A businessman, he had been brought into the Sultan's Government two years before as Foreign Minister. When I was shown into his cool air-conditioned office I was surprised to find such a young man, hardly more than forty. Dressed in a fine white *dishdasha* and turban, he spoke impeccable English with a quiet voice and smoked exclusive cigarettes in a holder. He got through the pleasantries quickly and then said, 'What do you need for your work?' I told him: 'A car, an interpreter, an office and a telephone.' I also explained that I thought it would be useful if I could have some sort of high-powered identity document explaining what I was doing and instructing any officials to render me whatever assistance I required. Zawawi arranged it immediately, sending copies with my photograph to each Provincial Governor and Head of Police. Later, that document was to prove a godsend.

Just a week later I set out on my first trip to the interior of Oman. All the country away from the capital, Muscat, is referred to as 'the Interior' or 'the Oman'. For centuries Muscat and Oman were separate and on occasion hostile states. One of Qaboos's first acts on coming to power was to change the name of his country from Muscat and Oman to simply Oman, in an attempt to end the age-old enmity between the people of the Interior and the coastal people who live round the capital. My introduction to the Interior was to start with Rostaq, a town about sixty miles from Muscat, and at one time the capital of the Interior. Malcolm Dennison called for me at the Annexe at eight-thirty the next morning. In future our starting time would always be shortly after six: that is to say, just long enough after sunrise to break camp and have a mug of tea. This is the army way of doing things, and it allows you to travel a good distance before the sun gets too hot; breakfast is taken mid-morning.

That first morning, I slung my canvas bag with camp bed, sleeping bag and bottles of the most powerful suntan lotion I had been able to find, into the open back of one of the Land Rovers, while Malcolm introduced me to our army driver and our cook. Malcolm would drive the leading Land Rover, with me as passenger, and the others would follow in the other. His reference to this second vehicle as our 'back-up Land Rover' was the first time that it dawned on me that making a film in Oman might really be more like organizing an expedition.

We plugged north-westwards up a tarmac road, straight and hot, passing mile after mile of construction sites interspersed with little villages built of odd timbers and palm leaves. The land was flat and sandy, dotted with stunted trees. Two miles away to our right was the sea, hidden from view for most of the time by a line of palm trees. To our left, shimmering in the heat like iron, lay a jagged line of mountains. This flat plain between mountains and sea is the Batinah. A thousand years ago much of it was under cultivation: now there is only the occasional government experimental farm where they are trying to rediscover what will grow and to find out how the ancient Persian settlers irrigated this barren land. We drove in silence. I tried to make conversation, but Malcolm Dennison seemed little inclined to talk.

After two hours we turned off towards the mountains. Now we were on a track, shuddering over loose stones, 'People warned me about the roads in Oman,' I said. 'Now I see what they mean.'

'Oh, no,' said Malcolm, 'this is still a main road. You'll know the difference all right when we get on to the second-class road.'

I wasn't sure how my spine was going to stand up to the continuous jarring if the roads got any worse. As we headed towards the mountains, the landscape began to change; there were no more straggling villages or herds of goats. Instead we saw camels in ones and twos chewing at the squat thorn bushes. As the ground began to rise, it changed from sand to rust-coloured jagged stones.

Malcolm Dennison had said 'three hours to Rostaq'. He and other experienced travellers in the Interior never refer to distances in miles. Exactly three hours after we had left the Annexe, we rolled down a dried-up river bed and into an oasis at the entrance to a mountain pass: Rostaq. On either side were thick banks of palm trees. Through them one could just make out the mud walls of houses in the shade. We pulled up beside two young men with rifles who were trying to repair a car. White-robed men came out of the trees to greet us. Malcolm is a celebrity in the Interior. Wherever he goes, word of his coming goes on before him, and friends come out to greet him the moment he stops.

We were led through the palm trees to a thick-walled house. Outside the *majlis*, or men's sitting-room, we took off our shoes. Taking off your shoes in an Arab house is not only a mark of respect; it has the underlying practical benefit of preventing mud and dust from being trampled into the beautiful hand-made carpets – traditionally the most valuable items in a house. Our host led us into the sitting-room, which perhaps was fifteen feet long and ten feet wide. The group arranged itself in a rough order of precedence: host and chief guest at the head of the room, servants nearest the door. Our host indicated that we should sit, and we squatted cross-legged on the Persian carpet, our backs propped on cushions against the wall. While Malcolm, the cook and the driver continued a ritual exchange of formal greetings with our host and his friends, I was able to look round the room. Beautifully proportioned, its walls were stone and mud, apparently held together with dried camel dung. It was impossible to judge its age, though it looked centuries old. It was covered with a sort of white distemper, and the roof, which seemed to be of plaited leaves, was supported by exposed, dark wooden beams. These were carved with geometrical patterns coloured blue, red and white. Deep windows with iron bars, but no glass, looked out into the shade of the palm trees. Inside it was delightfully cool, neither draughty like air-conditioning nor sweaty like concrete houses in such heat. The thick mud walls kept back the heat, while the windows allowed the slightest stirring of the cool air under the palm trees to pass through the room.

Trays were brought in and set on the ground before us. The plates were covered with what looked like straw teacosies. When they were taken off, tinned peach segments, fresh oranges and halwa were revealed. Halwa is the traditional Middle Eastern sweetmeat, looking like a brown form of Turkish delight. A Victorian missionary, Samuel Zwemer, described it in his book *Arabia, The Cradle of Islam*: '. . . halwa, which to the acquired taste is delicious, but to the stranger smells of rancid butter and tastes of sweet wagon grease'. I liked it, finding it similar to Turkish delight, but with a smoky flavour of nuts and spices. If you eat too much, it can give you the most penetrating indigestion.

As we were about to lean forward and plunge our hands into the communal bowls of food, Malcolm, who was sitting next to me, muttered, 'Only use your right hand – the left is for something else.' As soon as the covers were removed, flies settled on the food in droves, and although an occasional hand was flapped to wave them away, people on the whole seemed to accept them. Presumably they breed so fast in such heat that over the centuries men have become resigned to them. Although we never really got used to them, we found that with the passing weeks we too became much less inclined to waste precious energy chasing them off our faces or equipment. In spite of the flies, one of the things that immediately impressed me was the traditional emphasis on cleanliness. As soon as we had finished eating, a man came round with a jug of water and an aluminium bowl with a sort of strainer on top. He poured water over my hand until I indicated that it was clean. A second man came round with a towel so that I could dry it. Next came coffee, served not from an Arabian coffee pot but from a Thermos jug, black, unsweetened and aromatic. There were only three small cups, without handles, and everyone was expected to drink from them in turn. This is the normal practice in Oman. The man serving the coffee starts with the most important man in the room, and as each person finishes he passes his cup on to the next. Malcolm whispered, 'You must drink at least two cups. After that they'll try to give you more, but waggle your cup to stop it, and hold your hand up.'

All the time that this was going on people who had heard that Malcolm was in the town kept coming to greet him. Each time someone came in we all stood up, and the new arrival went round the whole circle shaking hands with everyone. Very good for the leg muscles. No women came, of course, though we could hear them chattering somewhere else in the house. Quite small boys were, however, welcome to join the circle. Later Malcolm told me that he had been visiting that house for over fifteen years and accounted our host a very good friend, and yet he had never seen his wife.

The local governor, the Wali, joined us for lunch. We had been there for about two hours, and the coffee and first lot of refreshments had been removed, when we were invited to step outside where a servant was waiting with a bar of soap and a jug to pour water over our hands so that we could wash again. Once we were seated again in the room, servants brought in two huge trays, at least three feet across. On each was a mound of rice topped with sauce and raisins. They were set down before us and bowls of chopped tomatoes and red onions were emptied over them. Limes were cut in half and scattered round the edges of the trays. Water was poured into our glasses. Incongruously, we were each offered a tin of Japanese tangerine juice. We gathered in two circles round the two huge trays, and the men who had been serving joined us – one of our strongest impressions of the Interior of Oman was the innate equality of traditional communal life, a life which we in Europe have long since ceased to understand. Our host tore apart the mounds of rice, and underneath each was a whole cooked goat cut into large lumps. He took a dagger and hacked succulent pieces off for us. Everyone started to eat. It is difficult to eat rice and chopped tomato with the fingers of one hand only – at least without spilling a good deal and getting food all round your face. I noticed with some relief, however, that even the Arabs were spilling quite a lot. Another hazard of eating with your fingers, I soon discovered, was that if you plunge your hand into a steaming joint of meat you burn your fingers. I never learnt to eat elegantly with my fingers while I was in Oman, in spite of the patient teaching of many Omani friends.

Meat is a luxury in Oman, and people eat mainly rice, fruit and vegetables. Chicken is becoming more common and is often served by thoughtful Omani hosts to visiting Europeans as they know we prefer it to the customary guest meal of goat. As most homes have no refrigeration, the only way to keep meat fresh is to keep the animal on the hoof. When guests arrive it will be killed and eaten immediately. What is left over, after the guests have eaten their fill, is passed on to the women and children of the household and then to others in the village. The most highly prized meat is camel, which is kept only for the most special occasions, and which we were never offered. Next comes mutton and then goat, followed by chicken or fish. Entertaining can be expensive, and many an Omani has been ruined by following the traditional code of hospitality too conscientiously – a single goat costs about £40 or $80! We met several formerly wealthy men who are now destitute because they had been unable to resist the traditional rules of hospitality, which demand that you provide the best for those who call on you. Their so-called friends had taken advantage of their good manners.

After our meal we had to go and pay our respects to the Wali. Normally we would have had to do this first, but as he had joined us for lunch we were excused. The order in which you visit people is important and can call for great diplomacy. Early one morning, for instance, we drove into a mountain village called Al Hamra. We drove direct to the Wali's house, but he wasn't there. While we were waiting for him to be found, a messenger came from the brother of the Sheikh (the traditional tribal leader of the village) inviting us to call on him and take coffee. Malcolm Dennison explained that we must wait and see the Wali first. After a while the Wali appeared, and we sat to take traditional coffee and refreshments. While this was going on another messenger appeared, from the Sheikh himself this time, asking us to take coffee with him. Although we had already spent over an hour drinking coffee with the Wali, it was not an invitation we could refuse. So we all proceeded round the village towards the Sheikh's house. On such an occasion not only the visitors from outside the village, but everyone who has been taking coffee, will move on to call on the new host. These processions through the villages always reminded me strongly of the traditional *Boy's Own Paper* picture of the founders of the British Empire. There we were, two white men preceded by guards with old British rifles – the Wali's Askars – walking sedately through the village, accompanied by a knot of white-robed Omanis. Whenever we passed a group of women they would stop drawing water or doing their washing and turn their heads away until we men had passed. Every so often a man would appear, and our procession would stop while everyone shook hands. On this particular morning in Al Hamra, our walk to the Sheikh's house took us past the home of his brother. Seeing us

approach, he assumed that we had come to take coffee with him and came out to welcome us. However, to have taken coffee with the Sheikh's brother before we had taken coffee with the Sheikh himself would have been a great insult to the Sheikh. It called for all Malcolm's persuasiveness and tact to extract us from this situation without giving mortal offence. Only after we had had coffee with the Sheikh were we free to be entertained by his brother.

All over Oman one meeting will lead to another. While you are sitting in one *majlis* someone else will appear and invite you to his. For Malcolm Dennison such meetings can be important. It is by sitting, talking to the men and taking coffee that he finds out what is going on in the Interior, who is plotting with whom, which tribe is about to quarrel with another. Over the next few days we were to meet a stream of people who came to Malcolm for aid and advice. The reason he is so loved is that he will listen to people's troubles, and if he can't help them himself he will try to get the Government to do something. On that first day at Rostaq he visited one old man who wanted a new well for his palm garden and tried to find work for another who had lost his job.

As the afternoon drew on, we pushed up into the mountains. They were of bare rock, mostly a rich rust colour, but with subtle gradations from pale sand-yellow through varied hues of blue to the occasional striking patch of purple. They were not rounded by glaciers or the gentle effects of rain, but sharp and jagged.

It gets dark very quickly in Oman, changing from afternoon to night in an hour. Malcolm turned off the track and headed into rough ground. The two Land Rovers pulled up thirty

Rostaq Souk.

Agricultural centre, Rostaq.

yards apart. Without instructions from Malcolm we all spread out and started to gather dead wood from the dried-out bushes for a fire. Our driver put up Malcolm's bed and set deck-chairs in front of our Land Rover (the front of which would serve as sideboard and dressing-table, the wing-mirrors as coat-hooks). They had travelled in the wildest parts of Oman for months at a time over the last fifteen years, and it was obviously a well-practised routine.

While the cook pumped the primus stove and prepared the supper, our driver brought over two steaming mugs of sweet tea. 'Very refreshing after a long flog,' said Malcolm, and he laced them generously from a bottle of rum drawn from a mysterious cardboard box that had been set down in front of the Land Rover. As we sat and sipped our tea in the rapidly failing light, jangled muscles started to relax from the shuddering journey and the rum started to seep into the stiffest corners. One of the Omanis was prostrating himself towards Mecca.

Relaxing in the growing dark with a man you have been sitting beside all day in silence – the roar of the Land Rover had made it impossible to talk – conversation becomes unhurried, relaxed and considered. By the time it is dark, the talk has become remarkably honest. During those evenings in the open, I came to trust Malcolm Dennison more than anybody else I met in Oman. Later, whenever things became fraught, it was always to him that I turned for advice.

The cook brought over our supper: a bowl of rice and meat stew. While we sat in our deck-chairs, the two Omanis squatted apart from us by the fire. Even out in the wilds, army routine applied: officers ate in their mess, by the Land Rover; other ranks in theirs, by the fire. Sitting separately also meant that Malcolm and I could drink alcohol without embarrassment. The cardboard box from which Malcolm had taken the rum also held bottles of whisky. Whisky has great medicinal qualities in a hot climate, and Malcolm, along with other old Oman hands, recommended it without qualification as the best way of killing the legions of virulent stomach bugs. We drank it with generous quantities of water. As Malcolm told me, visitors who put chemical purifiers in their water, or drink only imported bottled water, build up no resistance to the local bugs. Then, when inevitably they come into contact with untreated water, used to wash food or as part of a meal in an Omani house, they come down with a really bad bout of stomach trouble.

Malcolm Dennison is a man who has never liked towns. He was born in the Orkneys and plans to retire there. Certainly he seemed more truly alive living rough in the mountains and deserts of the Interior than in his pleasantly furnished house in Muscat. Although we did not post a sentry, our nights in the open followed a well-ordered military routine. Before sunset I had set up my small spring camp bed a few yards from our Land Rover, while Dennison's old criss-cross wood and canvas army bed was being set up by the driver a few yards away on the other side. The two Omanis would sleep on the ground by the fire, rolled up in a cloth or a blanket. At about half-past nine, by which time we had usually consumed about half a bottle of whisky, Malcolm would announce that it was time to turn in. There was no need for tents, of course, but during my first few nights in the Interior it got quite cold in the small hours and a heavy dew fell.

Later, when the film crew pitched camp, we had a number of adventures with scorpions, snakes and the notorious camel spiders, which are reputed to use fangs to anaesthetize the part of you they have taken a liking to, so that they can eat your flesh while you sleep. However, I had only one disturbed night under the stars while I was travelling with Malcolm Dennison – I suppose his experience taught him just where we should stop to avoid problems. That one night was, however, rather eerie.

We had turned in, a safe distance above high-water mark, on a sandy beach facing out on to the Indian Ocean. I dreamt – or assumed I dreamt – that a massive dog, a latter-day Hound of the Baskervilles, was walking, panting, round me where I lay. I woke, but could see nothing. I lay down and tried to get back to sleep, but after a few minutes the metal bed frame and taut canvas seemed to be throbbing, drumming. I sat up but could still make out nothing. The drumming stopped, but as soon as I lay down it started again. I lay there trying to make out what it could be: the only thing I could imagine was hundreds of ants, or perhaps termites, gnawing at the sprung metal legs of the bed. I shot bolt upright and gingerly peered over the low side of the bed. I could still see nothing. Tentatively I felt the legs and ran my hand over the sand under the bed. Still nothing, and again the drumming stopped.

Again I lay down and when the drumming started again I tried to put it out of my head. But the drumming got louder and I opened my eyes. I was lying on my side; there, not a foot in front of my face, just above the edge of the bed, was a pale shape with a pair of little eyes staring at me. It can't have been more than four or five inches across, but at that range and in my anxious state it seemed enormous. I reached my left hand surreptitiously out of the sleeping bag, found a shoe and took a wild swipe at the face. It went flying off the bed and scuttled away, sideways, across the sand, disappearing from sight behind some tufts of coarse grass.

When I woke next morning the sun was just climbing out of the glassy ocean. I sat up in the sleeping bag to watch the sunrise. Then I noticed around my bed large paw marks in the sand. When I told Malcolm about my experience he said reassuringly, 'Yes, I saw it. A wild dog came and had a sniff at you and then walked away. I thought you were asleep. Anyway, he wouldn't have touched you.' As for the pair of eyes belonging to the scuffling creature, Dennison was sure that it was a crab. They lived in holes all along that beach. Its claws had caused the drumming sound as it climbed the metal frame of the camp bed.

On Saturday, 5 April, I at last met the Sultan. I had flown south to Salalah, the capital of Dhofar Province.

Five hundred miles south of Muscat, I was struck by a heat fiercer than anything I had experienced in the north. The silver BAC 1-11 seemed rather out of place on an airfield where all the other planes, Hunters, Strikemasters and helicopters, were dispersed behind walls of sandbags. I had been told to expect to spend a day with the troops on active service before my audience with the Sultan, and had gone dressed accordingly. An ADC was to meet me on arrival and explain my timetable. Spotting among the crowd a young Omani officer wearing red lapel tabs, I approached him. 'Mr Darlow?' he said, 'I thought perhaps you hadn't come.' He led the way to an air-conditioned car and we sped into the town. 'You will see His Majesty in half an hour.' When I pointed out that I was dressed not for an audience with His Majesty, but for the battlefront, the officer said, 'I thought you looked a bit casual.' He said he would take me to the Palace guest house so that I could change.

We drove through the gates of the Old Palace in Salalah. Long breakers rolled up the perfect sandy beach, and, apart from sentries and some fishermen in a dugout far out to sea, there was no sign of life. The ADC led the way through an archway and up a flight of stone stairs. Inside ,two stout Askars, white-robed and armed with rifles, shuffled to attention. At the top of the stairs was a corridor and more Askars. I was shown into a well-furnished suite of rooms. The officer told me to change and said that he would be back when His Majesty was ready. I calculated that I had about fifteen minutes. While I was in the bathroom changing, a servant glided in with a tray of tea – China tea from a fine bone-china tea service, of a design that we would all soon know well.

The fifteen minutes lengthened into two hours. Eventually a policeman came and joined me. I assumed that he had come to take me to the Sultan, but he sat in the chair opposite me, looking out over the dazzling blue sea. We fell into conversation, and when he learned that I came from London he became quite sentimental.

He had recently returned from the Hendon police training college, and thought London a fine city and British policemen the best in the world. Now he had been appointed to the police detachment at the Palace.

After about fifteen minutes another officer appeared and said that His Majesty was now ready. With the officer walking in front and the policeman a pace or two behind, I proceeded down the stairs past the Askars and across a courtyard. We went under another arch and mounted more stone stairs. At each door there was a pair of Askars. At the approach of our little procession, they would shuffle to attention and greet us, bowing slightly. We climbed flight after flight of stairs. At the top of each one we came into the blinding sunlight of an open courtyard only to be plunged immediately into the dark of another staircase. It was a quite unreal sensation, winding one's way through alternate light and dark to the top of that old palace, and I lost all sense of direction. I had assumed that someone would brief me on the protocol for meeting the Sultan before I was taken into his presence, but as we climbed those stairs it became increasingly obvious that there would be no briefing. I had just decided to ask the officer what I had to do when we came out into the light of another courtyard. Deftly the officer turned aside, and from the dark of a doorway opposite I heard a voice saying, 'Mr Darlow, it is a great pleasure to see you.' As I walked through the door the Sultan held out his hand, a trim, neatly bearded figure in a simple white robe. All sense of awkwardness and formality was banished.

The officer, the policeman and the others in the room melted away as the Sultan led me to a small private cinema. His Majesty had asked to be shown one of my previous productions, and I had brought a film with me to Oman. As we entered, a dozen officers and members of his personal staff rose. He led me up a small aisle and invited me to sit beside him. The aides took their places on the other side of the aisle. His Majesty asked me to explain a little of the background to the film he was about to see. His most striking feature was his eyes, which looked as if he was always about to break into a smile. It is often said that his father retained his power for so long because his personal charm always disarmed his critics. Qaboos has certainly inherited that charm, even though his infinitely more enlightened policies mean he can put his personal magnetism to better use.

Once the screening was over, the Sultan asked about my plans for filming his country and what help I would need. I explained that I wanted to try to make a film portrait of Oman by looking at the lives of a representative cross-section of his people, rich and poor, in the capital and in the remotest parts of the Interior. We also discussed the best way of filming him. Normally, one might choose to interview the Head of State, but I felt that it would be more interesting if I could film him in an unobtrusive way as he went about his work. He agreed that I could follow him about his normal state duties for one or two whole days. The audience had lasted two hours.

I had been in Oman for almost four weeks. Now I could leave Richard Fawkes, who had that day flown out to join me, to continue the work of setting up the production, while I returned to London to brief the film crew.

The Capital Area

Carved door, Muscat.

YOUNG BOY, MUSCAT

KORANIC SCHOOL, ROSTAQ

KORANIC SCHOOL, ROSTAQ

CHILDREN, SUR

GUARD AT THE GATES OF ROSTAQ FORT

GUARD AT THE FORT, ROSTAQ

RELIGIOUS LEADER, ROSTAQ

A phone call in London, and within a week I was on my way to join Michael in Muscat.

Having used every wile at his command, he was by then installed in the Al Falaj Hotel proper, and I moved in to share a room with him. Accommodation in Oman is at a premium, and if either of us was away from the capital for a night, one of a succession of interesting foreigners from around the globe immediately moved into the spare bed.

I reached the hotel after midnight and spent

Young boy, Muscat.

the rest of the night discussing the progress, or more accurately the lack of progress, Michael had made, the places he had visited, and the shape of the film he proposed making. The speed with which I had been engaged as writer and co-producer, and had set out, meant that I was even less prepared than the director: a glance at the map to discover where Oman is, and a book to read on the long, leg-cramping flight.

Michael departed at dawn for Salalah and his audience with the Sultan, and I read through the notes he had left me ready for a meeting with Sayyed (which means 'Lord') Fahar, Minister of the Interior, Deputy Minister of Defence and uncle to the Sultan.

The purpose of the meeting was two-fold: to request the assistance of the Sultan's Air Force in taking us round the country, so that we could complete our research within a realistic timetable; and to discuss the country's defence policy.

Bait al Falaj, the headquarters of the Sultan's Armed Forces, is where Sayyed Fahar has his office. The whitewashed fort, with its limp flag hanging from a crenellated tower, and its surrounding cluster of colonial-style bungalows, nestles in the Ruwi valley only a ten-minute walk from the hotel.

The sentries sprang to attention and gave me a ramrod salute. They did not ask me for any identification, and indeed during the next two months I entered Bait Al Falaj regularly without ever being challenged. I can only presume that some strange logic says that a European is to be trusted. The sentries seemed most put out when I asked them the way to the Minister's office, and were relieved when a passing driver offered to take me.

In the office of the Minister's adviser – a

seconded British officer who was at breakfast –
I was asked to wait and offered a cup of coffee.
There were already two men in the room, an
Arab officer and a civilian. They said hello, and
carried on talking. Gradually the room filled up
with more officers, senior policemen and civilians,
until every available chair was taken and there
was no standing room left. There was still no
sign of the adviser, so the senior officer present,
a colonel, said 'Shall we begin?' and there started
a meeting to discuss a display of captured Russian
weapons. No one seemed to mind my presence,
and I sat listening as security arrangements were
discussed in detail. Later, whenever we needed
help from the top, I was to discover that everyone concerned knew me from this meeting,
although no one had been introduced and no
names had been mentioned.

When I eventually got to see Sayyed Fahar,
it was in his other office in the Ministry of the
Interior, further down the Ruwi valley and a
car ride away. He was happy to give us as many
planes as we wished, but refused to talk about
defence at all since it would have meant moving
back to Bait al Falaj: he likes to keep his two jobs
separate.

With Michael back in London, I was left to
continue setting up the shoot. Most of my time
was spent in Muscat itself.

There is only one road into Muscat, built as a
single track by the British Royal Engineers in
1929. Before that, the only way to reach the town
was on foot or by donkey over rough mountain
paths. The road climbs steeply up towards a
saddle in the jagged rocks, from which one can
look down on Muscat, crushed into its rocky
hollow against the blue waters of the Indian
Ocean. Watchtowers, like castles from a game of

The Main Gate, Muscat.

chess, sit on the surrounding pinnacles. Built
more than two centuries ago, they are so high
and inaccessible that long ago, when the last army
to invade the town reached them, it just marched
past, leaving the defenders powerless up in the
air.

The road descends steeply past the first
houses of the town which cling to the rock walls,
chunks missing from their walls where lorries
and cars have failed to negotiate the tight
bends, and past a well, a hole in the pavement
where decades of ropes have worn deep grooves

View of Muttrah.

The Main Gate, Muscat.

Muscat, street scene.

View of Muttrah.

in the wooden surround and where the colourfully dressed Baluchi women, today with plastic buckets and containers, still draw water, surrounded by petrol fumes and honking traffic. It is another two hundred yards from this well to the town wall, Muscat's main defence, but there is always a tail-back of traffic, for right outside the main gate, under a concrete umbrella, essential shade from the relentless sun, stands a policeman, whistle blowing and arms waving: Oman's only permanent traffic control. Pedestrians walk where they please, slowing progress down even more.

Rounding the policeman, one turns through the town's main gate, the Bab Kabir, with its heavy wooden doors, which were closed in Said bin Taimur's day three hours after sunset, signalled by the firing of a cannon. Once the gates were locked, no one was allowed to move around inside the town without a lantern (a torch was not permitted); and if your light went out, you were liable to spend at least the rest of that night in prison. There were originally only three gates into the town: the Bab Kabir; a small one for pedestrians and donkeys leading to the *Souk* or market quarter; and a third for larger vehicles, which before 1970 were allowed to travel only from Muscat to the commercial capital of Muttrah in the next main bay, and then only with special permission from the Governor. A fourth large gateway, with no gates, has been added recently to take traffic out of the town, for the Bab Kabir is only wide enough to take a single car and inside the wall the traffic flow is one way.

Muscat was never built with the motor car in mind. Inside an area smaller than Soho or Greenwich Village, but with twice as many buildings, alleyways twist and turn between massive dilapidated house walls of traditional Arab design. Here and there bulldozers have been at work, leaving empty spaces where boys play football, men lie sleeping or talking, and goats forage; some of these we saw munching happily on cement sacks, which must be a sure-fire remedy for the local stomach bugs. Soon office blocks and government buildings will rise side by side with the wooden shacks of the poor, and Muscat will resemble many another Middle Eastern town.

Dominating the view are the two romantic Beau Geste forts of Merani and Jalali, half a mile apart. At one time in their history, rival leaders sat in them and lobbed cannon-balls at each other, with a British gunboat there to see fair play.

In the shadow of Merani, which is being turned into a tourist attraction, stands a new and impressive mosque, a present to the people from Sultan Qaboos. Between the two forts, overshadowing the town and the waterfront, is a new Palace for the Sultan; and squashed into what remains of the waterfront and overlooked by Fort Jalali is the British Embassy, a fine old structure, once the most imposing building in Muscat. Its terraces are designed to catch the slightest breeze from the sea. The Embassy used to have its own jetty, so that visiting gunboat captains could come ashore for the night without technically ever setting foot in the Sultanate. Qaboos had it removed. The wooden main gates, varnish reflecting the sun, heavy brass studs gleaming from frequent polishing, look like part of a romantic film set. Above them stands a proud British royal coat-of-arms. What lies inside the gate is like a dream of Empire. The neat gravel forecourt leads to a front hall where

Young boy, Muscat.

Young boy, Muscat.

copies of *The Times* lie beneath a portrait of the Queen. A notice advertises a forthcoming Gilbert and Sullivan night, a production of *Trial by Jury*, and the walls of the stairs up to the terrace are lined with faded sepia photographs of every British agent, representative and ambassador to the Sultanate. Harassed members of the staff hold urgent consultations because they have overspent Whitehall's allowance for the Queen's Birthday party (held in the open on the only day of the month when it rained) by almost £1, and no one knows who will make up the difference.

Muscat has been the capital of the coast since the eighteenth century, but it is not really suited for the role. With no proper port facilities, no contact with the rest of the country until the road was built, no water within the town walls – as generations of defenders discovered to their cost – and no room for expansion, it is unbearably hot in the summer when the temperatures climb into the hundreds and refuse to fall. The mountains attract the heat and retain it. During the summer, residents use their hot-water tanks as cold, since they are inside the buildings, and the cold-water tanks, which stand on the roof, for hot water – except that during the day the water is too hot to use without scalding. At noon it is so still and hot in the town that the goats rarely climb on to the parked cars, as is usual, to reach the leaves of trees in the Old Palace gardens, but instead lie panting under lorries out of the sun. At sunset they emerge to climb the surrounding rocks overlooking the bay and stand silhouetted in the evening light like strange mythical figures.

Muttrah, Muscat's twin city in the next bay, has always been the commercial centre of Oman. Here a smaller replica of the Muscat forts looks down on an untidy town, teeming with people of every nationality who come there to trade. A strange walled area next to the *Souk*, a town within the town, is the province of the Indian-descended Hyderabadhi traders. They retain their own language and customs, and no one, not even the police, enters the square half-mile without an invitation.

Every type of face can be seen in the *Souk*, the largest in the country. The population of Oman includes Arabs, Zanzibaris, Indians, and Baluchis from across the Gulf. Shops, cafés and streets are crowded with goods, people and the sound of barter. Shopkeepers sit cross-legged at the tops of stone steps, inviting passers-by to stop and peer into the darkened caverns behind them. All the shop floors are at least three feet from the ground since the *Souk* is sited in a wadi or dry river-bed, and when the rains come it is awash with water rushing down to the sea.

Behind the *Souk* are the residential quarters of the town and a laundry that puts the clean white *dishdashas* on the rocks to dry. One day we looked up to see a black goat with dusty hooves walking across every single article. Between the town and the sea is the Corniche, a new stretch of two-lane road bypassing the town and linking Muscat with the Interior. At the northern end of Muttrah, the Corniche turns inland, past a café with the proud sign 'THE CORNISH RESTAURANT', and heads up into the hills, cutting through a man-made cleft in the rocks. To the right is a largely Baluchi-inhabited area of small mud-built houses and *barastis*, homes made from palm fronds.

In one of these *barastis* lives the Shadhad family, the family we chose to film as typical of the modern capital dwellers. A *barasti* is built like a stockade. Wooden poles form the corner-posts, and the walls are made from palm fronds either woven or tied together. Inside the walls a central courtyard is surrounded by rooms made in a similar fashion, in which the family lives, sometimes as many as four generations together. The dirt floors of the rooms are covered with mats and carpets, on which the family sit and sleep. Dust blows in through the gaps in the fronds, and *barastis* are impossible to keep clean. The walls are no defence against the processions of ants either, as we discovered when sitting there. Outside the Shadhad *barasti*, Isa, the twenty-one-year-old head of the household, had painted the words 'LOVE' and 'PEACE', and the international peace sign adorns their water tank.

Although most of the Shadhad family live in Muttrah, Isa's father is old and has a small market garden at Seeb, twenty miles up the coast, where he stays apart from the family. This arrangement, strange at first to Europeans, is common in Oman. The male head of the household will often travel to find work; or, if one of the children has to leave home, one parent will go with him or her to set up a second house.

In the absence of his father, Isa has become

head of the household. Although he has an elder brother studying in Jordan, he is the eldest male at home. Every communication to the family will automatically be made to the eldest boy, even if he is quite young.

Women in Oman, as in many places in the Islamic world, do not show themselves to strange men, and many houses have a separate entrance for women and female visitors. There is no hard-and-fast rule in Oman about the wearing of the veil, not an Arab custom but one imported from the Ottoman Empire. In some tribes the women remove their veils only in the privacy of the bedroom; and in others they half-cover the face or just pull a shawl across when a man approaches. The one universal tradition is that an Arab woman will wear black if she is going to be seen in public.

We met the Shadhad family through the police. Oman was the first Gulf state to introduce policewomen, because of the need to search women at the international airport, and among the first intake was Isa's younger sister Fawzia, aged eighteen. The move shocked her family. Her mother was horrified, her uncles, aunts and cousins were scandalized; not that a girl should work, for there is a saying, 'Omani women have the best manners of anybody in the world, and they work for their men like donkeys,' but that she should work with men. The vast majority of girl secretaries are Indian or from other Arab countries. It is now considered all right by many families for an Omani girl to become a teacher, provided she teaches only girls, or a nurse, so long as it is in the women's wards; but to work in the same office as men – and in Fawzia's case, to come into contact with male criminals!

Muttrah Souk.

Isa returned home from leading a Boy Scout delegation to Beirut to find his sister missing; she had joined the police and gone to their training school ten miles out of Muscat. Being a modern young man, he talked to Fawzia, discovered that her mind was made up, and agreed to support her against family hostility. As soon as their father heard the news, he came to the house and demanded the return of his daughter. He was under the impression that she was working for the money, which reflected badly on his manhood and ability to provide for his family. But when she took her parents to the training school and let them see that she was

MUTTRAH SOUK

MAN WEAVING, ROSTAQ

BULLET MAKER, ROSTAQ SOUK

KHUNJAR MAKER, SUR

ROSTAQ SOUK

Muttrah Souk.

happy in her job and that she was being well looked after, they agreed to let her stay. It was, in its own way, a dramatic break with tradition.

Although still with the police, Fawzia is now married. Her courtship with Suleiman, who works in the port as a truck driver, was not typical either. Suleiman, a cousin, was visiting the house when he first saw Fawzia and they fell in love. Suleiman was frightened to tell Isa, though Isa is the younger man, and Fawzia had to tell him. Since it seemed to Isa that Suleiman was not progressing with enough speed, he took him on one side and told him to take her to the pictures, at the same time giving him a stern warning to make sure he had her home by midnight. The customary manner of engaging and marrying is for the parents to negotiate on behalf of the children, often without the intending parties having seen one another. Obviously emboldened by the cinema, Suleiman took matters into his own hands. When his family visited the Shadhads for tea, Suleiman declared in a loud voice that he wanted to marry Fawzia. 'So I said,' Isa told us, ' "This is not the way to marry. Sit down, we are going to discuss it." Suleiman said, "No. I want to marry Fawzia. Do you like it or not? If you say no, I am going to leave the house – if you say yes, I am going to sit." So I said, "OK, sit." '

Visiting the Shadhad household, we were served water and coffee by Isa's youngest brother, aged twelve. 'We do this,' explained Isa, 'because in Oman we think that when young boys know how to bring water, how to talk and sit with people, they are going to be men earlier. Perhaps you come to my house and I am not here. My younger brother is going to bring coffee, tea and talk with you as a big man

because he knows how to talk with you.' Throughout Oman, very young boys would always join us in meetings with the men of the village.

Isa works in the Ministry of Education, in the department which deals with recruiting overseas teachers. For work he has to wear traditional Omani dress, and most days, when he arrives home, he changes into jeans and shirt. Fawzia, on the other hand, wears uniform at work and changes into Omani clothes as soon as she gets home. We got to know her quite well, and had a very successful morning filming her at the police station; but the day we went to film her at home, as soon as she had changed she refused to leave her room, and nothing could persuade her to be filmed in Omani costume. She was the only member of the family to be strange about us or the camera. We never found out why; we supposed that once at home, away from the modern environment, she had reverted to her traditional role.

Below the *barastis* is the beach where the Muttrah fishing fleet lands and auctions its catch. Alongside the fish market, where once the mountains fell sheer into the sea, the port of Mina Qaboos has been built, eleven deep-water berths enclosed in a breakwater of concrete structures, like hundreds of Henry Moore sculptures.

Formerly, all produce entering Oman was lightered from ships anchored either in Muscat or Muttrah bay. The cargo was left on the quayside and a businessman learnt strictly by rumour that his goods had arrived. He had to go to the quay, clamber over the piles of other cargo to locate his own piece, and clear it through customs himself. In 1970, with development happening so fast, a port was a

Muttrah Port.

Workers, Muttrah Port.

Dhow workers, Muttrah port.

major priority to bring in equipment, machinery, cement and all the necessary materials for basic projects. A small port had been started by Said bin Taimur after the discovery of oil, and it was greatly expanded by Sultan Qaboos.

The port has a policy of Omanization; since the new-found wealth of the country is supposed to be for the people, there is no point in importing all the labour from abroad. This in itself creates problems, which were explained to us by Joel Wilcox, the port director. An American, he is a member of a United Nations team sent in to set up the port ready to hand over to Omani management; the members of the team are the only foreigners working there.

'One of the problems in running a port,' he told us, 'is that it requires great physical strength. Bag goods don't lend themselves to mechanical handling the way that crates and cartons will. We find that a man from the Interior does not have the stamina, because up till now his diet has been principally rice and milk with a few dates. Meat is eaten only on festive occasions. The coastal and Baluchi labourers do have access to fresh fish, and so have more stamina. However, the development of the country is going forward at such a rate that we have a shortage of labour. For this reason we have to depend on anybody we can get, and nutrition does become a problem. With the affluence that comes with this high employment the younger children are getting protein in their diet, and I think the generation coming up will have much more stamina and be able to work longer hours in the heat.'

The majority of Omanis are not money-minded (the port has never had a strike for more pay). This unworldliness in itself makes problems for a modern port manager like Wilcox: 'A man sets a kind of mental daily goal: "I want to earn two rials per day." And when he determines that he has earned his two rials then he is through. He goes and gets cleaned up, goes over to the coffee shop and sits down and spends the rest of the day in gossip and the usual social intercourse with his fellow men. We have the problem, too, that every date tree in Oman is registered and belongs to someone. When the season arrives our people leave and go to pick dates. We have offered monetary rewards – if you stay on we'll pay you extra, we'll pay you double. The answer is almost routinely, "This is the one time of the year my family and I can get together, all of my cousins, uncles, aunts, brothers and so forth. And we all get together and we sing the old songs and spin the old tales and

re-live the old legends." They are not going to give that up. Really, looking at it from the standpoint of the nation, I think it'll be a sad day when they do give it up. Looking at it from the standpoint of operating the port, I wish they would.'

The problems of running the port are those of any big business in Oman, but it has especial difficulty in recruiting middle and junior management. A man with sufficient experience to become a ship's pilot, for instance, is in line for a very good job in the Sultan's navy. Similarly, a man who can read and write does not want to spend his days in a hot, airless warehouse as a tally clerk if he can get a job in an air-conditioned government office.

Outside the port, many menial jobs, especially on building sites, are done by immigrants from India and Pakistan; equally, almost the entire medical service is run by Indians and Pakistanis. The Arab tribes of Oman themselves are traditionally divided into three classes: a master or ruling class; a secondary class which includes the skilled craftsmen; and a third class who are the only ones to perform manual labour. One job which carries status, and which any Omani will do regardless of tribe or class, is driving, and a person in charge of anything that moves is called a driver. The drivers engaged by the port are like children with new toys. Frequently they go missing and are discovered out on the Corniche, racing from roundabout to roundabout, just for the sheer thrill of being in charge of a car.

Before 1970 there were a bare 200 vehicles in the Sultanate, these belonging mostly to the armed forces and the oil company. Now there are more than 25,000, mostly in the capital area,

Dhow worker, Muttrah Port.

If it doesn't start, well, then you find a shady place and lie down and wait for a passing caravan to come by and help you with your load. We've gradually overcome this, and they're now reporting when their fork-lift breaks down. They're beginning to recognize the symptoms that precede a breakdown. They're beginning to recognize the symptoms of running out of fuel. The training programme is beginning to pay off. I think by the time we reach the end of the United Nations contract we will have an efficient operation.'

The port is due to be handed over by 1977, and Joel Wilcox is hopeful that he will meet the deadline. Local managers are already in foreign ports, studying their methods, prior to returning to take over.

At Ruwi, in a once barren valley over the hills from the port of Muttrah, has sprung up the new administrative centre of the country. Ministries, embassies, shops, supermarkets, cafés, cinemas, houses, flats for government employees, and the Al Falaj Hotel, rise from a sea of building sites and trenches for drainage, telephone cables, water pipes and electric mains. Electricity and water cause the great headaches. There is one tiny generating plant for the entire capital area at the moment, and power cuts happen frequently, though fortunately each hotel room has a ready supply of candles! But these are the short-term problems that arise when decades of town planning and engineering are compressed into months.

Like any other modern town, Ruwi suffers from rush hours and traffic jams. Cafés with loudspeakers blare out Arab and Western pop music, and cinemas show Indian, American and British films and the ubiquitous Italian 'spaghetti

driven by people who until recently were more used to the closing and overtaking speeds of a camel. Accidents happen every minute of the day, and the most dangerous place to be is on the eighteen-mile stretch of road out to the airport.

The enthusiasm for things mechanical has not yet extended to an ability to rectify faults. When Joel Wilcox arrived, as he told us, 'Whenever a fork-lift broke down, the driver would figure, "Well, my camel died," and he would get off and kick it a couple of times.

Westerns'. The influence of these films is one of the explanations offered for Oman's crime rate. Not that crime was unknown before Sultan Qaboos; but in the old days bandits only robbed outsiders and never members of their own tribe, who were considered to be 'family'. Now that modernization is breaking down tribal patterns, the capital area is starting to notice mugging, pocket-picking and petty crime. The problem is very small by Western standards, but with the growth of urbanization it is only too likely to increase.

Oman's need for workers acts as a magnet for unemployed men from neighbouring countries, and she has a far worse problem with illegal immigration than Britain has. A sizeable amount of the national income is spent on rounding up, accommodating and repatriating those hundreds who are caught every month.

The eighteen miles from Muscat to Seeb International Airport will eventually be completely developed. By the side of the road, shells of factories, sites for stores, garages and housing schemes change the face of the landscape daily. On a rocky headland at Qorum, half-way between Muscat and Seeb, is a complex housing the Ministry of Information, a new museum of Omani history, and the radio and television stations. The television station is remarkable: seven months after the contract to build the station was signed, the site had been cleared, the shell of the building built, the transmitter installed and the station put on the air. The service, the first colour television in the Gulf, was opened by Muna Mafhoud, an Omani girl who had been the first female radio announcer. All the television announcers are women, on the direct orders of the Sultan. He realized that television would have an immense influence on his people, and he is particularly concerned with the emancipation of women. He wants to use television to educate and change the traditional attitudes of Omanis, helping them to adapt to modern ways, and he has installed public television sets in and around the capital. The most popular programme is the cartoon series *Woody Woodpecker*.

It is in the capital area that one sees the most marked signs of development, of the new wealth at work and the contrast between yesterday and today. Sandwiched between the factories and tented cities are the *barastis* of the local people, and rising from them are the television aerials. Women with water jars on their heads stroll to the wells, goats and camels wander across the road holding up the traffic, and children set off to school clutching outsize plastic briefcases. A man on a donkey rides slowly through the Bab Kabir into Muscat, ignoring the impatient hoots of the motorists, and stops to exchange greetings with the men sitting in the gateway – a symbol of Oman's growing-pains.

On the front at Muttrah every day can be seen a madman, a former policeman, still busy directing imaginary traffic. A few ignorant foreigners have been known to follow his directions and turn the wrong way up a one-way street into the *Souk*, but apart from them he harms no one and does no damage. He is fed by the people around him because they care about their fellow human beings. It is this traditional caring that is most under pressure from modernization and outside influences. How long will it last when it becomes easier to put social problems out of sight and out of mind, leaving the state to look after them?

The Batinah Coast

Suwaiq is about seventy miles north-west of Muscat on the Batinah Coast. We wanted to film the life of fishermen, and of all the fishing villages we had seen, Suwaiq was the most beautiful. The people of Suwaiq might resent the description of their town as a village, for although it holds only some 3,000 people, it is the capital of the area and the seat of the Wali, the provincial governor. All the towns of the Batinah Coast are beautiful, situated as they are on 200 miles of palm-lined golden sand, washed by the rollers of the Gulf of Oman; but what had attracted us to Suwaiq particularly was its unique combination of sand-coloured fortress, antique fish-market and pretty little mosque on the edge of the sea.

Suwaiq is not the biggest or most famous town on the Batinah Coast. That honour undoubtedly belongs to Sohar, which, until about A.D. 1100, was possibly the most important port in all Arabia. Sohar was the home of Sinbad the Sailor. In those days the town was surrounded by fertile fields, watered by wells and tunnels (*fālajs*) carrying fresh water from the mountains. The Persian author Hudud al-Alam, writing at that time, described Sohar as 'the emporium of the whole world; there is no town in the world where merchants are wealthier than here, and all the commodities of west, south, east and north are brought to this town'. Another writer described it as 'the hallway to China, the store-house of the East and Iraq, and the stay of the Yemen'. Sohar was reputed to have 12,000 houses, not built of mud and palm fronds but of brick and teak. It was the sailors and merchants of Sohar who were chiefly responsible for establishing Oman as a seafaring power. Strategically placed at the mouth of one of the great passes into the hinterland of Arabia, the Wadi Jizzi, Sohar was

the spot where the trade routes of the ancient world converged – the overland route from the Mediterranean and Baghdad, and the sea routes through the Gulf to India, China and Africa. Here the great ships anchored waiting for the winds to change. Today Sohar is not even a glorious ruin. It is a dilapidated little town, with ill-kept vestiges of a city wall, bordered on either side by silted-up creeks which must once have been its harbours.

We chose Suwaiq for its looks. When we asked Malcolm Dennison to introduce us to a typical fishing family, he advised us to contact Sayyed Fahar. Said bin Taimur had been suspicious of all the members of his family and had banished his brother Fahar to Suwaiq for thirteen years. On the face of it, it seemed unlikely that a member of the royal family would be the best person to introduce us to typical poor fishermen – a bit like asking the Prince of Wales to find a suitable Welsh miner – but when Richard approached Sayyed Fahar, he immediately volunteered to take us to Suwaiq himself.

Accordingly we climbed into a Land Rover at eight one morning, with Sayyed Fahar and one senior official to drive the two hours to Suwaiq. We went up the long straight tarmac road which runs the length of the Batinah Coast. Some ten miles before Suwaiq, Sayyed Fahar turned right on to a sandy track and headed towards the sea. We were soon passing through palm groves in which cattle grazed. Oman is reputed to produce the finest dates in Arabia, and the best of these come from the Batinah. The fringe of palm trees, varying from a few hundred yards to almost half a mile in width, runs almost without a break the full 200 miles of the coast.

Coming out of the palm groves, we found

ourselves in sand dunes some 300 yards from the sea. We turned left and followed a track running parallel to the shore. As our wheels slewed and spun in the soft sand, Sayyed Fahar explained that during the time of his exile in Suwaiq, and indeed up until two years ago, this track had been the only road along the coast; what had taken us just two hours used to take a whole day.

On the beach stood a village. We drew up on the far side on firm sand. The thirty or forty huts were made of leaves and wood that had been bleached by the sun to almost the same dull colour as the sand. Wooden dugout fishing boats and what appeared to be canoes made of reeds were drawn up in neat lines on the beach. Along the coast, stretching into the distance, were more lines of boats drawn up in front of other villages. Hardly had we stopped before we were surrounded by an excited crowd of men and boys. In the background women and girls peered from the doorways. The men immediately recognized Sayyed Fahar and burst into spontaneous rhythmic clapping, chanting and cheers. When he got out of the Land Rover the excited mob, many of whom removed their shoes as a mark of respect, crowded round him reaching out to clasp his hand or trying to kiss his feet. It was the most spontaneous outburst of enthusiasm for a ruler that we had seen anywhere in the world. In each of the villages we visited that day it was the same, and at one point, surrounded by a crowd of fishermen, he turned to us and said, 'How can they say our family is not popular? You can see for yourselves.' Sayyed Fahar was followed by a man handing out small gifts of money to the crowd; but not to buy their applause. As Sayyed Fahar put it to us, 'One must do a little to help these people, they are very poor. When you come here to work you should give everyone who helps you something, a bag of rice or some other gift that will help them along.'

In that first village, called Buday'ah, Sayyed Fahar asked the crowd around him to bring a fisherman called Salah to him. Salah appeared, a small, wiry, weather-beaten man with a ready smile. He greeted Sayyed Fahar as an old friend. He was instructed to clamber into the back of the Land Rover with us, and we sped off along the beach. By now the news seemed to be running before us and we hardly arrived in each succeeding cluster of huts before a crowd formed. At each place Sayyed Fahar stopped for a few moments to greet the people.

Eventually, we pulled up in front of the imposing old fort at Suwaiq. This is the seat of the regional governor, the Wali. The Wali is the Sultan's personal representative in the area and is responsible for administration and justice. The country is divided into some forty regions or Wilayats, ruled by Walis. It is a system which dates back to the time when Muscat and Oman were administratively separate. Oman, being a large and wild country with a scattered population, could not be effectively governed by one man from Muscat. So the Imams of Oman, the elected temporal and religious leaders of the Interior, appointed Walis with almost autonomous powers, which could be challenged only by the tribal leaders, the Sheikhs. Today, Qaboos has reduced the power of the Sheikhs in order to end the tribal rivalries which have so long riven Oman, and the Walis are the supreme power in their areas. As the country is opened up and communications are improved, the authority of the central Government becomes greater and the powers of the individual Walis become correspondingly less; however, they are still important men, and we could make no move without first securing their approval.

The gateway to the fort at Suwaiq was a graceful arch with two huge wooden doors which stood open. Beyond them the gatehouse ran back for some twenty-five feet before opening on to a forecourt. Built into the walls on either side of the gatehouse was a ledge which served as a seat. All over Oman there are similar fortresses, and wherever you stop you can see guards and casual visitors sitting in the shade of gatehouses, passing the time in endless conversation. We took up our station, sitting on the ledge inside the gatehouse, while an Askar, trailing his heavy rifle behind him, fled upstairs to find the Wali.

The Wali appeared, and greetings were exchanged. Then Sayyed Fahar told him not to let our arrival interfere with the proceedings of his court. As Sayyed Fahar did not wish to go up to the airless courtroom, the Wali obligingly transferred his proceedings down to us. While benches were being laid out in a line in the middle of the gatehouse, Sayyed Fahar indicated that we should sit beside him on the ledge and watch what happened. The Wali and his retinue took up their stations on the ledge opposite, while the people involved in the disputes sat on the benches in the middle. The gatehouse was thronged with white-robed men, many holding Boer War vintage Martini-Henry rifles elaborately decorated with silver. Beside the Wali sat the Qadi, a figure who looked like an Old Testament prophet. The Qadi is an expert in the Sharia or Islamic law. The prophet Mohammed laid down a code to govern all aspects of life, not merely the religious; and the Koran and the Sunna, a collection of sayings traditionally attributed to the Prophet, form the basis of the law practised daily

in modern courts. In each province there is a Qadi who sits to advise the Wali on the interpretation of the law. In Oman there are no lawyers' fees, and in the rare event of a man disputing the judgement of the local Wali and Qadi, he is free to appeal himself to the central court in Muscat whose president is nominally, and often in practice, the Sultan himself.

We had arrived in the middle of an extremely acrimonious marital dispute. Soon the case was proceeding as if we had not been there. Yet our presence must have been hard to ignore, as not only were they now arguing in front of a member of the Royal family, but the duties of hospitality had to be carried out while the case continued. So, as the husband and his wife's father screamed abuse at each other, servants carried round an enormous bowl of fresh halwa, plates of dates and glasses of water and coffee.

As is the way with Omani courts, everyone present was soon involved. The case had apparently arisen because the bride had left her husband's house and returned to her father. Her husband was demanding that she be returned to him. The Wali pointed out to the father that as the husband had paid a proper dowry for his wife, the father had no right to keep the girl with him. However, at this point a woman's voice broke in. Women are not allowed in the court; but just outside the gate, sitting in the dust, were two women completely encased in black, presumably the bride and her mother. The bride was screaming at the top of her voice and everyone in the court seemed very shocked by what she said. Sayyed Fahar explained: 'She is saying that her husband came to bed with her drunk.' Sayyed Fahar turned on the woman and said, 'You must not say such things here. It is not the business of the whole village what a man does in bed with his wife.' But the woman, far from being intimidated by this reprimand from a member of the Royal House, turned a stream of complaint on Sayyed Fahar. For a while everybody shouted at once. Then, in an attempt to calm things down, the Wali instructed two of his men to take the father round a corner out of sight. Sayyed Fahar explained to us that they would tell the man quietly that if he did not hand his daughter over at once he was liable to be sent to prison. The way Sayyed Fahar put it, it sounded rather ominous to our Western ears. However, far from being cowed, the father returned more adamant than ever. He didn't care if they sent him to prison, he was not going to hand his daughter back to this awful man.

We never did discover what happened in the case, because soon after that Sayyed Fahar said he had seen enough and got up to leave. Although the Sultan greatly wants to improve the lot of women, it will be many years before traditional attitudes are much changed.

We came to have considerable respect for the Walis' courts. They were informal and often chaotic, with everyone shouting at once; nevertheless, everyone did have his say. In one respect they have a better chance of reaching the truth than our own courts: there is no rigid formality of procedure to inhibit or intimidate or cut short those who have something important to say. Contempt of court would seem to be unheard of, and the exorbitant costs which prevent many ordinary people from going to law at all in England are unknown.

Sayyed Fahar took us to many villages around Suwaiq, introducing us to the people and showing us the way they lived. When he asked us which ones we most wanted to film, we chose Buday'ah (the first we had visited) and Suwaiq itself. Before we left he instructed Salah and the Wali to see that we got all the help we needed. Our only cause for regret was that there was no way we could persuade Sayyed Fahar to pay a return visit while we were actually filming.

When we returned to Suwaiq with the crew it was our first expedition out of the capital area. For the first time we were travelling in full convoy, with three Land Rovers and a Chevrolet truck full of stores. In addition to the film crew, we had four drivers, an interpreter and a cook. It is worth saying a little about each of them, as they were to become major characters in our adventures. First the drivers: Abdullah, Ahmed, Salah and Nasser. We had asked for Omani drivers because we didn't want to exhaust the crew with long hours of driving. We needed people experienced at covering long distances over rough unsignposted tracks and with enough mechanical knowledge to keep the Land Rovers going in the event of a breakdown. Abdullah drove the lead Land Rover. A quiet young man, always dressed in an immaculate *dishdasha*, he turned out to be our safest driver and our most reliable mechanic. Ahmed was a cheerful, bandy-legged little man who we immediately guessed must have been in the army. He spoke some fractured English and often helped with interpretation. Salah (not to be confused with Salah the fisherman) was a big man who invariably wore sunglasses – the Omani equivalent of a wide-boy. Nasser was a thin little man who drove the truck. He had a strange grin, a high-pitched voice, and spoke no English. The other drivers said that he was a little touched

51

in the head. Our interpreter, Abdullah Hamed, was a jolly young man whose friends ascribed his rapidly increasing girth to the amount of beer he drank. He had travelled a lot in Europe, but found that he was not made for the rigorous life that we were to lead, and soon left us. Finally there was our cook, Ferdinand, a gentle little Indian who could speak neither English nor Arabic. He had literally only just stepped off the boat when he was told to join us. It is doubtful if he had any idea what he was stepping into. It seemed that he had a cousin who already had a job in Oman, who heard that there was a job going connected with the Palace and sent him a letter telling him to come over on the next boat.

We had chosen Suwaiq for our first nights away from base because it was only two hours' drive away and if the worst came to the worst we could always go back for the night. Although the material we were to shoot in Suwaiq and Buday'ah was a vital part of the film, we at the same time regarded our visit as something of a training run for the longer expeditions ahead.

We decided to do as we had done on our visit with Sayyed Fahar, and headed first for Buday'ah. We made the two-hour journey without incident and drew up in the village. There we picked up Salah and drove on to report to the Wali at Suwaiq. The Wali had promised to find us somewhere to camp. After greeting us and entertaining us to coffee, he proudly led us up a steep slope to the inner keep of his fort. The inner keep was an open space some thirty yards square surrounded by a wall with a tower at each corner. He led us to a small open sitting-room which he had had painted specially for our arrival. 'This will be your *majlis*,' he said, 'and you can sleep in the courtyard.' There was also a separate room for Ferdinand to use as a kitchen.

We had arranged with Salah that we would visit Buday'ah late that afternoon, to make plans with the villagers for filming next day, so we decided to unpack our equipment and arrange our camp in the fort immediately. As we chose spots for our beds we realized that from the walls we could look down on the whole of the town of Suwaiq. Behind us we could see beyond the palm groves to the mountains of the Jebal Akhdar, while in front of us stretched the beach and Indian Ocean. It must have been one of the most romantic places ever devised for a camp, and we thought of the huge sums tourists would be willing to pay to stay in such a spot. Only perhaps the more pampered of them might have shared our mounting doubts about the cuisine as we started to unpack the stores loaded on to the Chevrolet by the Palace Provisioner. We had naïvely assumed that the Omanis with whom we were working would be far more used to living rough in their own country than we were. It was not simply that the food that we humped off the Chevrolet consisted of some sacks of rice, some cans of luncheon meat, and box after box of tinned orange juice, but that there was no can opener – not even a kitchen knife big enough to pierce tins with – and no proper cooking implements at all. There was, however, a complete dinner service of Japanese bone china, identical to the one from which Michael had drunk tea in the palace at Salalah. It is hardly surprising that it did not survive a trip to the Interior: what is surprising is that it got to Suwaiq at all. There were six Chinese hurricane lamps, without oil, and, although they were still in their boxes, the glass in all but one was broken. Luckily, Suwaiq is

Fishermen, Suwaiq.
Father and daughter, Suwaiq.

a market town, and we were able to get enough for Ferdinand to knock up a meal. It all seemed a romantic adventure, and everyone took our misfortunes in good part.

Late that afternoon we drove three miles down the coast to Buday'ah, where we were met by Salah, who had called the villagers together so that we could tell them what we wanted. In the middle of the cluster of huts, carpets, which had been brought out of the houses, were set down in the dust in the shade of a palm-frond wall. Having taken our shoes off, we all sat in a line and waited for the people to gather. We became aware of rustling noises from the wall behind us and dimly saw the eyes of little girls peering at us through the slats. Slowly the men of the village began to gather. As each appeared we all stood up, and they shook our hands in turn. After about half an hour there were perhaps a hundred men and boys. Although Buday'ah is a poor village, they brought trays of oranges and packets of nuts to set before us, and we took coffee together. Michael asked Abdullah Hamed to thank them for receiving us and to say that we wanted to film them and their village, so that we could show the people in our country how they lived. Salah reminded them that we had come from the Sultan and that we had been brought to the village by their friend Sayyed Fahar. The elders of the village – there seemed to be no single sheikh or acknowledged leader – said that as we came from the Sultan they would give us anything we wanted: 'We will give you our lives,' they said.

To make sure that there had been no mis-understanding, we explained that if we were to show the way they lived, the way they brought up their children, the way they cooked, the things they ate, that would mean entering their houses and filming their wives. When this was translated there was consternation. Salah spoke to them, trying to encourage them, reminding them that it was the will of the Sultan. But the men would not be budged; they weren't going to let us see their wives. Then Salah spoke up again. He told them proudly that he was more loyal to the Sultan than they were, and so he would himself invite us to film in his house.

After the meeting we suggested that it might be a good idea to show our camera to the people in the village, so that they would know what to expect when we came back next day. Many of them had obviously never seen a camera before, but they must have heard what it did, because in no time there was an excited crowd running about clapping and generally showing off in front of us. Apart from the matter of the women, they were obviously eager to help, and one man in particular kept miming the way he fished. He repeatedly dived off the side of his boat into the sand and pretended to be swimming with his net, rounding up the fish. The general excitement infected the women of the village as well. Slowly they came out of their houses and began to edge towards us. Although the women never came right up to the camera, their daughters did eventually join the little boys playing in front of us, though each time we turned to face them they ran away giggling in a mixture of fear and excitement. It was like an elaborate game of 'Grandmother's Footsteps'. Finally the men gathered round the village poet, who extemporised a song for us: 'All praise to Sultan Qaboos.'

At 5.20 the next morning we set up our camera to film the sunrise. A few of the fishermen were already preparing their boats for the sea, but most of the village still seemed to be asleep. But the sun was like an alarm clock. As it pulled itself clear of the sea, the fishermen came out of their houses and started manhandling their boats down to the water's edge. The boats were of two sorts: slim wooden dugouts, painted fore and aft, driven nowadays by an outboard motor; and small rafts made from the stems of palm leaves sewn together with string. Some of these too have outboards, but most are still propelled with oars or by a sail. Because we were filming for the Sultan, each fisherman attached an Omani flag to the bows of his boat. The result was that when the fleet of twenty or thirty boats set out, it looked less like a poor Omani village going off to fish than the start of the Venice Regatta.

Peter and Michael scrambled into one of the dugouts to go out with them. At first it seemed very precarious, perching with the camera on a piece of wood level with the gunwales. A few hundred yards from the shore one of the boats pulled up a wicker basket, similar to a lobster-pot. This was a fish-trap, called a *dubai*. It had twenty or thirty brightly coloured fish in it, none of them species familiar in Europe. In addition to these the fishermen regularly catch shark, tuna, stingray, swordfish and sardines. We sailed on, pulling out more *dubais*. The fishermen started to cast their nets into the sea. However, after two or three attempts it was clear that they were only doing it for our benefit. There were no shoals of fish about that morning which they would be likely to catch in that sort of net. We moved further out to where they had laid an elaborate trap. This was a circle of nets anchored just below the surface and running down to a depth of perhaps twenty feet. The

circle was open at one end. The technique seemed similar to that used by Mediterranean tuna fishermen. The fishermen drew their boats up round the outside edge of the circle, and then one man from each boat dived in and took hold of the net, gathering it into an ever smaller circle. As the circle shrank, the fish rushed to break out and so wedged themselves in the mesh of the net. Then the fishermen pulled out the net, piece by piece, shaking the fish to the bottoms of their boats.

The fish that the villagers do not want for their own consumption they land at Suwaiq to sell at the fish auction. The auctioneer sits at the edge of the *Souk* nearest the shore. Round him gather fishmongers from Suwaiq and others who will take the fish to sell in the towns of the Interior. The fishermen lay their catch in the sand in front of the auctioneer. He is paid a commission by the fishermen in return for selling the fish and maintaining the price. By nine o'clock at the latest, all the fish will either be on sale in the *Souk* at Suwaiq or on their way by taxi, Land Rover or donkey to towns and villages further inland. In the old days, most of the fish sold in the towns away from the coast would have been dried, but now enterprising fishmongers have got themselves Land Rovers or hired taxis so that they can sell the fish fresh.

Apart from fish, the other component of the economy of the Batinah Coast is the date palm. The villagers grow more than enough dates for their own needs and sell the rest. However, the palm provides more than dates. Its fronds are the main material used in building the villagers' huts and for constructing the fishermen's rafts. The ribs used for the rafts are soaked in the sea for some days. Then the fishermen arrange them on the ground ready to sew together. The ribs are gathered to a point at either end to form bow and stern. The stems are pierced with an awl and a piece of coarse twine is drawn through. To give the rafts a keel, heavy rocks are placed along the centre line during construction. The method seems to have remained essentially unchanged for thousands of years; the principle is the same as that of the ancient Egyptian boats on which Thor Heyerdahl based the construction of his raft *Ra*.

It was Salah who had promised to show us his house, and accordingly, late in the afternoon, he invited us into the women's quarters – literally the harem. We ducked through the door into an open yard. There, sitting dutifully in the sand, were his women: his wife (just one: only wealthy men can afford more), his mother, his son's wife, his four daughters and his son's daughters. None was veiled. There too were his sons, his son's sons, his chickens and his goats. He described the different parts of the house for us. 'There are four living places, living quarters for summertime and living quarters for the winter. A sitting-room for the men and a sitting-room for the women. There are two doors: one door is to admit visitors, and the other door is for the use of close relatives and the women.' The kitchen, we discovered, was not under cover, though it did offer some shade; it was occupied by a calf.

We talked to Salah and established that he had nine children, five sons and four daughters. When we initially asked him how many were in his family, he said, 'I have five children,' and pointed to his sons, and it took several minutes before he agreed that he also had four daughters. We asked his eldest son, a fisherman, about the fishing, and it emerged that they could not make

an adequate living from fishing alone and so he had to go abroad to work. When our interpreter, Abdullah Hamed, asked him why he worked abroad rather than in Muscat, the son's reply was, 'I have tried to find work in Muscat. In fact I tried for a whole month but was always told, "Come back again next week".'

Before we left Buday'ah, the men of the village said that they wanted to show us their sword dance. This was a great honour, because the dance is normally performed only on special feast days and at the end of the fast of Ramadan. Each village has its own subtle variations, but essentially the same dance is performed all over Oman.

Although the Sultan has instigated archaeo-logical digs and wild-life counts in an effort to preserve the heritage of Oman before it is destroyed by modernization, no one seems to have made a proper collection or study of the country's folklore. A country isolated for so long from the outside world, without the polluting effect of radio, must have an unequalled treasure of songs, stories, epic poems and dances. Many must go back to the time of the Prophet, and some will probably stem, unaltered, from the heroic age of myth itself. No one seemed to be able to tell us with any certainty about the origins of the sword dance. The Europeans that we spoke to did not understand the words that were sung as an accompaniment; and the Omanis seemed so surprised that we should want to know that they appeared incapable of offering a translation of their own. The sword dance is almost cer-tainly a ritual re-enactment of tribal wars of long ago, but beyond that one cannot go.

At Buday'ah the men formed up in two opposing lines. The only instruments were two

OLD MEN, ROSTAQ SOUK

GUARDS, ROSTAQ FORT

THE WALI OF ROSTAQ

LOADING PROVISIONS, ROSTAQ

GUARD, ROSTAQ FORT

Children, Suwaiq.

Arab drums, but everyone joined in the singing. The men held on to each other and advanced, conga-like, with a halting step. Pairs of men, one from each line, took it in turn to take the swords. The pair would fight, leaping high in the air with bloodcurdling cries, or crouching and lunging with the sword. The aim was to cut one's opponent's thumb. There was a referee on hand with a goat-stick to part the men, as the fighting often got out of hand, the combatants rolling in the sand more like wrestlers than swordsmen. The unruliness of the dancing in Buday'ah, although it added a great deal of natural charm to the proceedings, was in itself a measure of the lack of sophistication of the village. When we saw the same dance performed at Sur, there was none of the uncontrolled wrestling, nor the same eagerness in the swordplay, and the steps had a more recognizable rhythmic pattern. Many times while we were in Oman we heard music coming from houses where there were wedding feasts. During the days before the bride is taken to her husband's house, the women dance. Try as we might, we never managed to watch this. It is also said that there are occasions when men and women dance together, but we never met a European who had seen this for himself.

As we were packing our equipment to leave Buday'ah, a deputation of men approached us. 'You know the Sultan, you must take a message to him for us. Tell him we need a new well in the village and we want a school built for our children.'

'Your request must be passed through the Wali,' said Abdullah Hamed.

'No,' said the men. 'We have helped you, now you must help us. Take our message to the Sultan – a new well and a school!'

The Sultan

'Before Qaboos, nothing.' The phrase was repeated many times by many people. It is difficult, if not impossible, for an outsider to believe what life in Oman was like before Sultan Qaboos's accession in 1970, and if we had not heard such similar stories from very different people, we might have thought them guilty of exaggeration.

Qaboos's father, Sultan Said bin Taimur, ruled Muscat and Oman for thirty-eight years. He inherited a poor, bankrupt country, in debt to foreign powers, including the British, and at everyone's beck and call.

On the death of Sultan Said bin Sultan in 1856, his two sons had divided their rule between the wealthy island of Zanzibar, an Omani colony, and Muscat. This agreement was formalized by the British in the 1861 Canning Award, under which, in return for independence from Muscat, Zanzibar agreed to pay her an annual sum. Deprived of the trading wealth of Zanzibar, Muscat and Oman hovered on the verge of bankruptcy, and the island's subsidy became a vital part of the Sultanate's income. British involvement in its payment also became an important factor in controlling the rulers of Muscat.

Until the discovery of oil in the mid 1960s, the only state revenue came from the Zanzibar subsidy, the selling of oil prospecting concessions, and a customs duty imposed on all goods being moved from one area to another. Some idea of the poverty of the country can be gleaned from the fact that in 1932, when Said bin Taimur came to power, the Sultanate's total budget was around £50,000.

Said managed to drag the national economy into the black, through a mixture of parsimony and astute book-keeping. He refused to build hospitals, or to permit schooling other than in the traditional Koranic schools where a child would learn the Koran by rote. There were no roads, no communications of any sort, no vehicles except for those belonging to the oil company and the armed forces; villagers were not allowed to travel outside their villages without special permission; and countless other petty restrictions were imposed. No foreigners except for oil company employees and seconded British officers (no Omani could rise above junior non-commissioned rank) were permitted to enter the country, and *their* movements were strictly controlled. Throughout his reign he personally administered everything that happened in his country, and he kept an iron grip. He effectively cut Oman off from the outside world, and his subjects lived as their forefathers had for centuries. 'To visit Oman then,' we were told, 'was like climbing into a time machine and travelling back to the twelfth century.'

Naturally, such a style of ruling was not acceptable to many of his people, and the last twenty years of Said bin Taimur's reign were marked by tribal revolts and bitter conflict as discontentment grew. If an Omani wanted education, he had to leave the country to find it, and once he acquired it, the Sultan would not allow him to return. Many Omanis abroad began to plot his overthrow. He distrusted education, knowing that to provide even the most rudimentary schooling in the Sultanate would not only cost him money but force him to import foreign teachers with their own ideas of nationalism and equality. 'The British lost India,' he was once quoted as saying, 'because they educated the people.' He was determined that he would not lose his kingdom for the same reason.

Said bin Taimur was a well-educated, travelled man with the charm characteristic of the family. It is said that when the British agent used to call upon him to deliver rebukes from Whitehall, the Sultan would discuss cricket so entertainingly that only when the audience was concluded did the agent realize he had forgotten to convey His or Her Majesty's displeasure.

Some say he governed on the age-old principle of 'divide and rule'; others that he was a guardian of tradition who was attempting to preserve the best of the Omani Islamic way of life. Whatever the guiding factor, he never questioned that his way was right and that he was the only person who knew what was good for his people.

The discovery of oil might have been expected to change Said's attitude towards finance; but it took five years from the first find for oil to be exported, and he wanted to wait until the cash was in his hand before starting any development. He announced a grand plan, including much-needed hospitals, schools, ports and government buildings; but he refused to reveal it to the men who should have been responsible for carrying it out. When his son, Qaboos, took over, he discovered that the plans for a small hospital at Ruwi did not include any provision for equipping the building or hiring staff to run it.

Said had become a recluse in his later years. Increasingly inaccessible even to his closest advisers, he had retired to his palace at Salalah, and rarely emerged. Rumours spread that he was already dead, to be countered by other rumours that he was on his palace roof with a telescope watching for people breaking any of his quirky and arbitrary laws, sending out his guards to arrest offenders and to throw them in gaol.

In the 1950s, supported by the British, he managed to put down a rebellion in the northern Interior led by the religious leader, the Imam. However, the rebels regrouped in Dhofar, and exploiting the injustices of his rule, they persuaded the proudly independent Dhofaris to join a new revolt. By the end of the 1960s the entire country was on the brink of civil war.

Finally, Qaboos decided that the time had come to act. Helped by British officers in the Sultan's army, he took over from his father in a bloodless coup on 23 July 1970. Said bin Taimur abdicated after his guards had been overpowered and he had been cornered in the recesses of his labyrinthine palace. Wounded in the foot by a shot from his own revolver, the ex-Sultan was hustled out of the palace, put on an RAF plane and flown to a dignified exile in London, where he died three years later.

Qaboos bin Said was born at Salalah in 1940 and educated privately by a tutor, and then for two years at Sandhurst. After a six-month posting with the British Army in Germany, he embarked on a world tour with one of his father's advisers and returned to Oman in 1964, where he was placed under immediate house-arrest at Salalah by the Sultan.

The takeover was a popular move. In the north the people celebrated their release from oppression; and for many of the rebels, who had been working for the removal of Said bin Taimur, his departure signalled the end of their revolt. Qaboos's mother is a Dhofari, and identifying himself with Dhofari aspirations, he immediately made an emotional appeal to the rebels to lay down their arms and join him in building a new nation. He promised sweeping reforms, removed the petty restrictions and announced a crash programme of development. He also made a call for all Omanis in exile to return and work for their country.

From the Gulf, from East Africa, from Zanzibar, from all over the world, Omanis returned and swore allegiance to the new Sultan. The first reforms removed most of the major grievances of the Dhofaris in particular, and only a hard core of Communists, pledged to overthrow any form of monarchy in Oman, were left to fight on. Backed by China and Russia, and operating out of the neighbouring People's Democratic Republic of Yemen, they still continue guerrilla warfare against the Omani Government.

The takeover is always referred to as 'the Revolution', although it was far from being a revolution in our sense of the word, since one autocrat replaced another and the style of government did not alter. What did change radically was the attitude of the monarch to his people. Qaboos's presence has united the country as it has not been united for hundreds of years, and he has given his subjects a glimpse of a better life, a life they could barely have conceived only five short years ago.

We had been trying for some weeks to arrange a day's filming with the Sultan. Then, one day, the phone rang in the hotel and it was Major Salim Ghazali, liaison officer between the Palace and the Ministry of Defence, to tell us that he had made arrangements for us to film His Majesty visiting two schools, one for boys and one for girls.

Accordingly, at six in the morning, we were at the training school for boys who intend to join the Sultan's armed forces, about twelve miles out of Muscat. The school staff had been warned that we were coming, but not that the Sultan would be there; that day we were the only people outside his immediate circle who knew his movements in advance and we were sworn to secrecy about his visit. They had been told that we were making a film about education, a fact that surprised them since only the week before they had been filmed by a genuine team from the Ministry of Education.

We wanted to film the Sultan arriving at 6.30, and so were anxious to stay as close as possible to the school entrance. Qaboos is a sensitive, reserved man who does not relish ceremony and pomp, and we particularly wanted to film him at a school because he seems most relaxed when with children or villagers, or out in the field with his troops. So that we could obtain the most natural film possible, Michael had agreed that we would follow him like a news-film crew, and not ask him to repeat actions or do anything special for us. We could hardly start the day by asking him to drive up a second time if we missed his arrival.

By the time the headmaster arrived, his deputy had finished showing us round the buildings and we were beginning to watch the clock. We insisted that the head should show us round a second time, asking for locked rooms to be opened in case something inside should be vital to our film. By half-past six we had looked at everything twice, and talked to the headmaster about his theories of education, and we could think of no legitimate excuse for not filming. Only there was no sign of the Sultan. Then Peter Middleton suddenly had the inspiration that we were waiting for the vehicle bringing the lights, which must have broken down.

'Don't worry,' said the head, 'we have lights here.'

'We also need some cables,' said Peter.

'We have those too.'

'But,' said Peter, thinking fast, 'we need special plugs, obtainable only in England.'

'Oh,' said the headmaster, and wandered off to his study, leaving us standing in the dehydrating sun, already high in the clear sky.

Almost an hour later we heard the sirens. Over the brow of the hill came a red Mercedes, flanked by police cars, leading a convoy of fast-moving vehicles. We braced ourselves, making a last-minute check that the camera was connected to the battery and the lights were working. The convoy flashed past. The Sultan was driving himself and had missed the school!

By the time he had gone half a mile down the road and turned round, the school was in panic. Everyone had seen him and knew he was on his way. The headmaster had changed his shirt and as he rushed to the entrance, ready to greet Qaboos, he said to us, 'You're very lucky, you'll get a bonus for your film. He's bound to come here.'

The Mercedes pulled up at the entrance and Qaboos climbed out. Small, lithe, his dark beard flecked with grey, he was immaculate in army uniform, every inch a monarch. Even when looking stern, his dark eyes betrayed a hint of humour. He did not acknowledge us but shook hands with the headmaster and immediately plunged into a tour of inspection. He visited every classroom, asking the boys questions, missing nothing. When a teacher asked his star pupil to read, Qaboos stopped him and pointed to a boy at the back. The boy stumbled through the passage; Qaboos encouraged him to work harder for his own sake and for Oman. From the classrooms, he went to the living quarters and the kitchens, the assembly hall and the staff room. As he moved from building to building, soldiers and Askars heavily armed with modern weapons took up positions outside. The Askars, dressed in traditional costume, were obviously selected for their loyalty rather than their martial skills. Several of them were a trifle overweight and looked distinctly uncomfortable at having to rush everywhere. We had been advised not to be too conspicuous with our gun microphone until the bodyguard had grown accustomed to us. When we put on the first clapper-board, the snap of the top arm hitting the board caused several guns to swing round.

The visit was over in half an hour. The entourage leapt back into their vehicles, the Sultan climbed behind the wheel of his car, which had been positioned for him, and the convoy shot away.

We sped back along the road to the capital. We had received orders not to follow the convoy, which had gone to a nearby army camp, but to go straight to the girls' school in Muttrah and wait. They had no advance warning of the visit, and we had to wait outside, not producing a camera until we heard the sirens. There was no shade and no breath of wind to relieve the oppressive heat, and the Land Rover was like a furnace. Behind the girls' school is the British Council building, and we wandered up to look at it, past the playground of the school where several small boys were playing football, one or two of them in *dishdashas* which they pulled up every time they made a run with the ball. In Said bin Taimur's day there was a national football team which had to play in traditional dress. Most of their games were against super-fit Arabs who had fled the revolution in Zanzibar and who played in proper soccer attire. Needless to say, the Omani side always lost by a considerable margin.

At last we heard the sirens, snatched up the camera and were ready to film as the Sultan's car turned the corner. As soon as they saw him the girls went wild. They left their classrooms and poured into the entrance hall, surging forward to touch him, screaming with delight. For those girls, aged between twelve and sixteen, he was as much a hero as a pop star is to Western girls, and the staff were just as enthusiastic. Qaboos was nearly pushed over in the crush, and escaped to the safety of the headmistress's office, while the reluctant girls were shepherded back to their classes.

By the time we emerged into the sunlight, word had sped round Muttrah that Qaboos was at the school, and a large crowd had gathered. The cheers that greeted his appearance were obviously genuine. In the figure of Qaboos the country has been united for the first time in centuries, and we saw plenty of evidence of his popularity. His greatest asset in ruling his troubled land is this love, and several people confided to us that he needs to get out and meet his subjects as often as possible: difficult, perhaps, for a man of his shy temperament, but essential to nurture even further their present affection.

With a wave of acknowledgement to the crowd, the Sultan climbed into his car and moved off. We had been told originally that here our day with Qaboos would be finished. However, he was clearly beginning to enjoy himself and sent word that we should follow. Something

like fifteen cars made up the convoy. First and last were two police cars, sirens wailing, lights flashing. In between came the Sultan's own Mercedes; his personal Askars, squeezed into a Cadillac from which at least some of them could never have emerged in a hurry if there had been a crisis; cars for his aides; Land Rovers crammed to overflowing with armed soldiers; and an ambulance just in case of emergencies. On the road, all other traffic must pull into the side and the drivers get out and stand by their vehicles until the convoy has passed.

None of the Sultan's harassed aides had any idea where he planned to take us, and, although we had obtained permission to travel inside the convoy, word had not filtered down to the policemen in the last car, who insisted we follow them. Since Qaboos was making lightning visits to schools and government buildings, for the first few stops we arrived as he was on his way out. We were not helped by the last police car stopping to check the driving licence of a parked truck driver.

The Sultan had taken the road into Muscat. By following the crowds we managed to catch up with the convoy outside another girls' school. Peter leapt out with a camera and ran after the leading cars. Rounding a corner, he had to jump back for his life. Qaboos had taken a wrong turning, executed a sharp turn and was heading back, throwing us and everyone else into utter confusion. As he passed Peter, he noticed him, smiled and shrugged his shoulders, as if to say 'I don't know where I am either!'

By this time he had relaxed visibly, realizing that we were simply following him with our camera and would not be asking him to act or to repeat movements. He had entered into the spirit of the filming, turning his best profile to the camera, moving himself into the light, slowing down his pace so that Peter could get in front of him.

The Sultan lives for much of the year in his palace at Salalah. When he visits Muscat his arrival is viewed with some apprehension by Ministers and government officials, because they never know when to expect him or what he will demand to see. And he always requires exact and prompt replies to his questions.

After visiting a fourth school, Qaboos made another quick about-turn and drove back around the outside of the town wall. There was pandemonium as his convoy followed suit, and once again we were left way behind. Ahmed, however, was determined to show us that we were right to have chosen him as our driver. He went off like a greyhound. The convoy had turned through the main gate into Muscat, and we screamed at Ahmed who we thought was heading straight back to Muttrah. He had us fooled. At the last moment, he swung the wheel and we scraped through the narrow gate on two wheels.

The Sultan had stopped outside the Diwan, the Ministry of Palace Affairs, housed in the former palace of Muscat. On his way in he was approached by a woman who had been sitting on her haunches, covered from head to foot in black. She had a grievance, and we were told she had been waiting to see Qaboos for two months to present a petition.

All subjects have access to their monarch, but the dictates of security, and the time-consuming demands of modern government, mean that in practice this is becoming more and more difficult. So the woman outside the Diwan

was fortunate. While she was ushered into the Sultan's presence, we waited outside with the soldiers and guards until a message was relayed to enter and film the meeting. The woman stated her case at great length, the Sultan listened patiently. The woman insisted. The Sultan cut her short. 'Tomorrow they will settle your matter.' And the woman, who had been crouching at the Sultan's feet, bowed herself out.

The Sultan is all-powerful: his word is law. He has to answer for his actions to no one. He rules by decree, and by meeting his people to sort out their problems. He cannot do all this completely on his own, and has appointed a cabinet of Ministers to help him. Although the Ministers are powerful men, they must refer all major decisions to the Sultan for approval. Such an approach has considerable advantages in a society which needs to move faster than any other the world has known: no long-drawn-out committees, no endlessly sending back plans for revision. If the Sultan says something must happen, it does, and with the minimum of delay.

But all the same, the lack of experience in working in a modern state that appears in most areas of Omani society is to be found at governmental level as well. When Qaboos took over, few Omanis had held positions of responsibility. There was only one qualified Omani doctor, and he returned from abroad to become Minister of Health. The most successful Omanis were the businessmen also working abroad; he had to persuade these men to return to form his government.

While the audience with the widow was in progress in the Diwan, we explained our problem of being so far down the convoy to one of the aides. He agreed that we should travel immediately behind His Majesty's car, and sent a corporal to inform everyone. The policemen looked very put out.

From the Diwan, the Sultan led us to his new palace being built on the waterfront. Like a flattened mushroom, it dominates the skyline and the town. The design is functional, for on the flat roof is a helicopter pad. We were not allowed into the palace; he had only gone in to change his shirt.

Back on the road, the convoy pulled out of Muscat and made towards Muttrah. In spite of our negotiations, the official photographer was determined not to allow us in front of him and had managed to block us. Going up the steep hill out of the town, his car stalled and we were forced to stop. The Sultan didn't notice and went driving on. In the time it took to restart the offending car, he was out of sight. The guards and soldiers held up behind us looked distinctly unhappy at being separated from their leader and were making threatening noises. As soon as they could get past us, they were away in hot pursuit of the Sultan.

We finally caught up with them outside the Secretariat building in Ruwi, the building which houses most ministries. Again we waited outside, because we had been told earlier that he was disturbed by rumours that government employees were using office time to conduct their own business, and that he intended paying a lightning visit to the offices which he did not want us to film. A flustered aide came running out; Qaboos had noticed that we were no longer with him and was concerned in case we had lost our way. We were quickly ushered into the building, to meet up with His Majesty just as he was expressing his displeasure at the long hair of one of the office boys. It was disgraceful, he told the trembling youth; if he was going to work for the Government, he must maintain standards. When he noticed a cigarette end on the floor, one glance and someone hurriedly picked up the offending stub.

The Sultan finished his tour of inspection and walked down the steps to his car. Another female suppliant moved forward and was reassured in a word that her case would be heard. She thanked him profusely and touched her hands to her eyes, a gesture that said she knew she was in the presence of her king.

He climbed into his car and sat for a moment motionless. His aide came trotting over to us. 'His Majesty says, "Thank you very much," he said, 'he is now going home for lunch and suggests that you do the same.'

With the sirens wailing and lights flashing, the convoy moved off, and the Sultan had gone.

Director of Education for the Sur region, Ahmed Ghazali.

Sur

Sur, at the farthest eastern tip of Oman, was once a great city. It was, so legend has it, the original home of the Phoenicians. In the nineteenth century it was probably the greatest centre of the slave and gun-running trades in the world. It has always been independent in its outlook; and to this day, with none of its grandeur left, this fishing and boat-building port of 10,000 people is proud of being different.

Although Sur is only a hundred miles down the coast from Muscat, it takes ten hours' hard driving to get there. Sur was to be our first long expedition, and we knew we had to set out early and well prepared. A small incident that marked the start of our journey may not seem worthy of note, and we did not see its full significance until later. Our drivers had been told to report to the hotel at six o'clock sharp, so that we could load the vehicles and check that everyone had water and spare cans of petrol before getting away to an early start. Three of the drivers arrived in good time, but little Nasser was late with the Chevrolet. By the time he arrived, the other drivers were taking a second breakfast in the hotel restaurant, and Nasser wanted to join them. Michael ticked him off and told him that as we were already behind schedule we must leave at once. All four drivers began to argue with each other in Arabic. The argument became so heated that the restaurant manager came over and asked us not to bring them in again. It seemed a trivial incident at the time, and we set off without another thought.

Our route to Sur was on rough roads all the way. South of Muscat the mountains drop straight into the ocean, and there is no coast road. First we had to head west, inland, then turn south for some hours, and only finally turn east and head for a mountain pass that would bring us back to the coast and down into Sur itself. The journey would take us over three mountain passes in all and alongside the infamous Wahiba Sands. Malcolm Dennison had impressed upon us that it is vital to keep in convoy over such country, and Michael had instructed one person in each Land Rover to check every few minutes that the vehicle behind was still there. Sometimes this could be very difficult, as the great cloud of dust thrown up by the wheels stretched back for hundreds of yards. But it is essential in these temperatures that, if someone has to stop, help should be forthcoming without delay. Stories of people dying from dehydration, particularly after an accident, are too frequent to take chances. The other danger is that after a breakdown people walk away from their vehicles to seek help. In the open glare of the sun, with the heat reflected back from the bare rocks, they may soon collapse. If they are not found in an hour or two they will be dead.

A French construction company was building a new road through the Interior to Sur, and our plan was to join them at a point where the new road runs close to the old route. After some four hours' driving we came upon their construction works. It was an awe-inspiring sight. All around as far as the eye could see were jagged, iron-coloured mountains through which the new road was being cut in a straight line. Running away into the distance was a grey ribbon dotted with bulldozers and dumper trucks. To house the workers the French had built an enormous air-conditioned settlement, like a holiday camp in the wilderness. The French foreman seemed glad to see visitors. Enveloped in dust and shouting through the roar of mechanical diggers, he invited us to lunch. We declined, with some regret; we had to press on.

Ebra is the only town of any size on the journey to Sur, a scattered oasis lying in a fold in the mountains. It was here that our first serious misfortune befell us. One of the drivers, Ahmed, had not seemed too happy when we started, but we thought that it was the prospect of being five days away from his family. As we went through Ebra, the third Land Rover in the convoy, Ahmed's, was missing. We stopped to allow him to catch up, but after five minutes there was still no sign of him. We turned back. After a few minutes we saw the Land Rover approaching, but Ahmed wasn't at the wheel; it was being driven by Bob McShane. Ahmed had developed a fever and then stopped to be sick. He was very proud of his position as a palace driver, and so Bob and Peter knew that there must be something seriously wrong when he allowed one of them to drive. Fortunately, there is a hospital at Ebra, so we were not far from help. The doctor on duty was an Indian woman. She prescribed a number of pills and said she thought he would be fit to continue the journey. But hardly had we got out of the hospital drive, than Ahmed was violently sick again. This time he was taken into the hospital on a stretcher, and there was no doubt that he would have to be left behind. The doctor expected us to leave someone with him (normal practice in Oman), but as we were already without our interpreter we could not spare anyone. We promised to pick him up in five days.

By now it was well on into the afternoon and we were barely half-way to Sur. We still had to pass the Wahiba Sands, not a place one would choose to get stranded for the night.

Leaving Ebra you can see the sands glowing bright gold on the horizon miles before you reach them. As we approached, it was like drawing near to a furnace. A dehydrating hot breeze blew off the dunes and across the road. Not a place for a breakdown. The sands themselves came to a surprisingly abrupt end as though the dunes had been piled up by a giant bulldozer. At the bottom of the slope there was a distinct line, and golden desert sand gave way to pale, almost grey grit and stones.

An hour and a half later we were past the sands and stopped by a roadside well for water. It was five o'clock; could we make it over the final treacherous pass and down into Sur before sunset? The drivers did not want to go over the pass in the dark as it meant driving over lava boulders and along river beds. But there seemed to be no alternative. We didn't know the tribes or the Wali in this area, and didn't want to pitch camp on unfamiliar territory. It seemed better to push on. As long as nothing went wrong, we ought to reach Sur just before sundown.

As we reached the top of the pass the sun was just dipping behind the mountains to our left. In front of us lay the headland on which stands the city of Sur, and the sea beyond was a fading grey line in the rapidly advancing twilight. An hour or so later we were picking our way in the dark towards the government compound where the Wali of Sur had made over an empty bungalow to our use. It had a living-room, one small bedroom, a shower room and a kitchen. Its greatest asset was a generously sized refrigerator; its greatest drawbacks were that it was built of concrete and that the air-conditioning was not working. So, while we could entertain visitors to cans of iced Coca-Cola, we dared not invite them to sit in the house for any length of time for fear they might wilt in the heat. We found that the best way of getting cool was to lie in the sea. Three hundred yards from our bungalow, hundreds of crabs played on the rock ledges that dropped straight into four feet of calm cool water. There are reputed to be sharks and giant rays off Sur, but we never saw any and floated in the sea with perfect confidence. One afternoon we had the experience of swimming among a shoal of giant turtles, gentle creatures that seemed unconcerned by our presence.

The government compound at Sur contains the school, the hospital, and bungalows for officials, doctors, nurses and teachers. In the bungalow next to ourselves lived the matron of the hospital, an American missionary who now works for the Government. In the days of Said bin Taimur, the only proper public hospital in the country was the American Mission Hospital in Muscat. Although these Christian missionaries have been in Oman for many years, they seem to have made no converts; they seem content to serve the people through medicine. Our neighbour on the other side was a nurse with the Save the Children Fund. As well as vaccinating children and combating disease in the Interior, the fund has mother-and-baby clinics in three of the principal towns. Once they have established a clinic and got it running properly, they hand it over to the Government so that the Omanis can run it themselves. Save the Children then moves on to establish a new clinic somewhere else.

The most numerous inhabitants of our compound were teachers: Egyptians, Jordanians, Palestinians. When Qaboos came to power, there were only three schools in the whole of Oman, with a total of 800 pupils. All were primary schools, and for boys only. The only form of education was the Koranic school, where bright children might pick up the art of reading by long hours of chanting from the Koran. Anyone who wanted his children to receive secondary education or professional training had to send them out of the country; and, once educated, they were not allowed back. Colonel David Smiley writes of asking Said bin Taimur about providing schools. 'Where would the teachers come from?' asked Said. 'I cannot afford to pay for teachers from England, and so they would come from Cairo and spread Nasser's seditious ideas among their pupils. What is there here for a young man with education? He would go to the University in Cairo or to the London School of Economics, finish in Moscow and come back here to foment trouble.'

Sultan Qaboos has changed all that. He has given education an even higher priority than medicine, and now every town of any size has its school, even though the classrooms may be marquees and the teachers still have to live around them in tents. One of the most appealing sights in all Oman is small boys with huge briefcases converging from all the points of the compass on their school. Walking in groups or singly, big children holding the hands of smaller ones, riding two and more on the back of a donkey, standing crowded into the backs of Land Rovers, they come in across the sands, over the rocks, down the valleys. These are a new generation who are aware that they have been held back by their lack of education, and they have an unquenchable thirst for knowledge. In the five years since Qaboos came to power, he has opened schools for 35,000 children, 8,000 of them girls. But it

A MOUNTAIN VILLAGE IN THE JEBAL AKHDAR

NEW ROAD INTO THE INTERIOR

SUNSET OVER THE JEBAL NAKHL

THE JEBAL NAKHL, IN THE INTERIOR

PALM GROVE, SUR

SHEPHERD WITH FLOCK , IN THE INTERIOR

Dhow builder, Sur.

takes time to create doctors and nurses, engineers and teachers, in a country where only 5 per cent of the population can read. Where it takes only a few years, if you have the money, to build hospitals, factories and schools, it takes generations to develop a population capable of running a modern state for themselves.

Qaboos has never shared his father's fear of the effects of education. Having no trained teachers of his own, he has to import those outsiders whose alien influence had so much alarmed Said bin Taimur. We spent one afternoon with a group of such teachers – Jordanians who were living in our compound. The full heat of summer was beginning, and they were living six to a room. They invited us in, and we sat on the beds discussing the future of Oman: 'They're trying to advance hundreds of years in a generation, and they cannot fail to have difficulties on the way. But we hope they make it.'

The person at Sur who interested us most was Ahmed Ghazali, the Director of Education for the region. A young man educated outside Oman, he lives in the compound with his young wife and two children. They live like Europeans. We visited his house more than once, and each time his wife would serve us tea or cold drinks and then sit with us to join in the conversation.

However, Richard glimpsed a black-clad figure in another room – Ahmed's grandmother. Ahmed apologized that she would not join us and explained that the old lady strongly disapproved of the way his wife entertained men in the house.

Both Ahmed and his brother Salim were rebels before 1970. Their father had left Oman so that his children could be educated. It was Malcolm Dennison who first introduced us to Ahmed, and it was he who told us their story. In the 1960s Ahmed and Salim, like so many educated young Omanis, wanted to return to their country but could not. The only hope for them, and for their less fortunate countrymen, seemed to be a change in the Government. In waiting for what they believed inevitable, they occupied themselves as best they could abroad with progressive politics, looking only for an opportunity to return home. When the old Sultan was overthrown, in July 1970, Ahmed was one of the first young Omanis to be given an audience by Sultan Qaboos. He was appointed to run a new school on Masirah Island off the south coast. It was the first school to take girls. From there he was transferred to become Director of Education at Sur, and he is obviously marked for an important career. Meanwhile his brother Salim contacted Malcolm Dennison and offered to return, with a group of previously hostile exiles, to work for the new Sultan. However, the authorities were still suspicious of his political background and were not ready to take him on trust as they had Ahmed. He was asked, as a token of good faith, to return without conditions and surrender himself to Malcolm Dennison. Salim did this and for two years worked under Dennison's supervision in his office. Now he has more than proved himself. He

holds the rank of major in the army, and we had met him as liaison officer between the Sultan himself and the Ministry of Defence. Their father also has now returned to Oman and holds the post of Head of Protocol in the Ministry of Foreign Affairs.

This family background would have been enough in itself to make a good subject for our film, but the work Ahmed Ghazali has done at Sur is so interesting as to make it unique. He is a man driven by a fervent pride in his country and a passionate concern for its people: 'As a nation we are starting from zero. But His Majesty has given us the opportunity to work, and he has called for every Omani to come back here and work. I don't think there is any justification for anyone not coming home and working for their country. I consider that every day that passes represents many years and so we must press on and work even harder. First we must restore the spirit of cooperation and unity which once made our nation powerful. It is important to understand that there is no material development without the development of human beings.'

Ahmed himself was our guide at Sur, once the most important centre of dhow-building in Arabia. While we were there, only one new dhow was under construction. The men who build them learn their craft from their fathers, and will tour the Arabian seas as far as India and Africa to find work in their traditional trade, moving from one job to another, as word reaches them of where a new boat is to be built. At Sur there are no indigenous trees, except a few palms which are not suitable; so all the wood has to be imported from India. The dhows are built with traditional hand tools – no power saws or electric drills. They can be eighty to a hundred

Dhow Building, Sur.

Dhows, Sur.

feet long and may take six months to build, but there are no plans at all: the construction is done completely from long-gathered knowledge. The hundreds of pieces of wood are fitted entirely by eye, and when the dhow is launched, it will float exactly true.

Sur is surrounded by water, and the smallest sound travels far. One day we heard quite clearly the beautiful rhythmic chanting of a work-song as men scraped the upper quarters of a dhow lying well out in a creek. On another occasion we listened as two men sang a question-and-answer song while they hauled bucket after bucket of water from the sea with which to swab down the decks. From the distance we heard the call of a muezzin, and, turning, saw a yellow-robed figure framed in a small arch under the white dome of a mosque some hundred yards away. The man seemed somehow too big for the arch, and the effect had the same charm as the out-of-proportion paintings you see in medieval manuscripts. Alas, by the time we got close enough to film he had disappeared.

One morning we went to the prizegiving at the local school. The ceremony started at eight o'clock with marching. Led by the Boy Scouts,

Dhow builder, Sur.

Old man, Sur.

Young boy, Sur Mosque.

the children paraded for the raising of the national flag in the school courtyard. To us all this martial pomp seemed rather uncharacteristic of Oman, but Ahmed assured us that it was nothing of the sort, and in line with the policy of trying to instil a corporate sense into the pupils. Then followed the prizegiving itself. The prizes were handed out by the Wali to girls as well as boys, and this seemed a much more warm-hearted Omani occasion. The prizes were not elaborate; rather they were educational or useful: pens and packets of toothbrushes and toothpaste.

Ahmed showed us round the displays that had been arranged in the classrooms. He drew our attention particularly to the exhibition of handicrafts done by the girls. He was proud of having over 800 girls attending school in the Sur region, but, he told us, 'It is not our primary intention to educate women so that they should go out to work. That is up to them. The important thing is that women must be educated. The idea behind the exhibition of handicraft is to show the parents that their girls are equipped to be good and experienced housewives in the completest sense, and that they are not merely taught how to read or write. Through education a girl is more likely to secure a happy future for herself and at the same time will be better able to create a happy environment for her husband and her family. Everything which takes place in the schools, including sports and handicrafts, has the aim of creating the best type of youth, young people who will choose to occupy their time with worthwhile activities rather than waste their time. Will four or five hours at school every day be enough to protect the children from the influences of the outside world where most of the people are uneducated? We

have to find ways of protecting our pupils from the harmful effects of that outside environment.'

Ahmed introduced us to a group of girls who, having reached the age of eleven, were about to leave primary school. We asked each of them if they would now settle down to becoming wives and mothers. Every single one wanted to go on for further education and follow a career. Most wanted to be nurses or doctors, but one girl's ambition was to become Oman's first woman petroleum engineer. Ahmed told us that, although these girls came from enlightened homes, it was very unlikely that all of them would be allowed by their fathers to receive further education, let alone go out into the world and take a job, until enlightenment had spread still further.

Ahmed stressed that the Government cannot achieve everything at once, even if it could afford to; the people must set about improving things for themselves. He has encouraged villages in the district to collect together and clear the ground where malarial mosquitoes breed, and to put into the water systems fish that feed off the mosquito larvae. He has got them to improve their own roads. He took us to a women's centre just outside Sur. There, he had encouraged the villagers to form a committee to raise funds and collect equipment to start evening classes for women. There were no government funds for this, but Ahmed was able to persuade some teachers to help. One of the men in the village gave over part of his house, and now women meet three evenings a week to learn to read and write, to do first aid and simple hygiene, to learn better ways of using materials and how to provide their families with a balanced diet. When we arrived many of the women wanted

Khunjar makers, Sur.

to leave, frightened of what their husbands would say if they knew that they had allowed themselves to be seen by strange men. But Ahmed told them that we had come on the orders of the Sultan and they must not leave. When the centre was first proposed, many husbands were against it, not wishing their wives to go out in company or become too independent. Now that it has been running for a year, they find that their wives cook and look after the family better and they have dropped their opposition. However, there is a new complaint – the women discuss subjects that their men don't understand!

Education and training are obviously the key to change and progress in Oman. Qaboos cannot wait while the new generation of children grow up; he has to train the adults to take over modern jobs. This doesn't mean simply retraining them in modern skills, it means giving them a complete education from the very start. For us, long used to literacy, it is easy to forget that almost every action in the running of a modern industrialized society depends on someone's ability to read, write and do arithmetic. When Qaboos took over in Oman, fewer than one person in ten could even write his name. Only fifty people altogether had the equivalent of a university degree. The only way that Oman could make progress was by starting a massive campaign of adult education. So now teachers not only run the schools on a shift system during the day, one set of pupils in the morning and another in the afternoon: they spend their evenings teaching the children's parents.

Perhaps Ahmed's most daring innovation at Sur has been to organize public meetings in mosques. Initially the idea was greeted with suspicion that amounted to hostility. Ahmed wanted people to be able to question their religious leaders on the Koran and the Islamic way of life. He believes that faith and progress should go together. The first of these meetings, late in 1974, was such a success that all the mosques now vie with each other to hold similar gatherings. A transcript of the questions and answers is published by Ahmed's Education Department each week and avidly discussed by groups of men as they take their coffee. Sur is probably the only place in the Moslem world where such public question-and-answer sessions are held.

One evening we were invited to one of these meetings in the biggest mosque in the town. By the time we arrived about two hundred men were sitting on the floor between the pillars in the main body of the mosque. Facing them in a line were four religious leaders and some of the Sheikhs. There were no women present, so we were particularly interested when one of the questions asked was, 'What is the attitude of Islam towards the education of women?' This was the complete reply:

'Islam is anxious that men and women should work together to complete the structure of this Islamic nation, and that woman shall not sit idle and fail to perform her role in society alongside men. Islam has given women their further rights. In pre-Islamic time woman was a mere possession; in Roman society, for instance, she was a neglected creature. But Islam came and established her rights, giving her the same rights as man, making education a duty for boys and girls alike. To prove this the Prophet has said that education is a duty for all Moslems, male and female alike. The Prophet has also said, of his wife Aisha, "Learn your religion from this redheaded woman." So I tell you that any man who neglects the education of his daughter will be punished by God for disobeying his rule. The Prophet has said. "Whoever has been given daughters by God and looks after them by educating them and providing for them, will be shielded by them in the second life from the life of hell." So I say to you, my brother Moslems, our female population represents half, if not more than half, of our nation, and so we cannot impose a life of ignorance and darkness upon more than half of our nation, chaining them down in our houses and never allowing them to take part in the activities of our country. So I urge you, educate your daughters for the glory of our country and for the fulfilment of God's will.'

Ahmed Ghazali has a healthy impatience with bureaucratic delay, and it is in character that he has turned down offers of promotion that would lead to a desk job in the capital. He prefers to work in direct contact with ordinary people. Because he was unhappy about the length of time it sometimes took to get government action on local problems, he persuaded the Wali of Sur to set up a council, composed of the Sheikhs and local officials. The council would have three functions. First, it could take action in local matters where there was no action from central Government in Muscat. Secondly, by representing a wide range of local opinion, it could bring pressure to bear on the Government for effective action. Thirdly, it would encourage the spirit of independence, collective decision-making and open discussion. When he first suggested the idea, the Wali was in favour but the Sheikhs were against. They were frightened of such a novel way of doing things because it seemed to challenge their individual authority.

Nevertheless the council was set up. After only a few months of operation it is a great success, and the Sheikhs join in its discussions as enthusiastically as anyone else. We attended a meeting where, first, a new syllabus for Sur schools was agreed; then there was a very lively discussion about government aid to local fishermen. It seems there is great resentment that large boats, equipped with refrigeration, come and poach the fish from Sur. This is then taken back to ports in the Persian Gulf or dumped on the Sur market, depressing the price of the local fishermen's catch. The council ended by telling the Wali in no uncertain manner that the Government was not doing enough to prevent this, and insisted that he take the matter up with the authorities in Muscat as a matter of urgency.

It may be recalled that our drivers had had a quarrel before we departed for Sur. The repercussions of that argument did not become apparent until the end of our visit. It was Friday, the Moslem day of rest, and we had given our drivers the day off. We were in the central square at Sur, filming a sword dance. Suddenly the Chevrolet truck driven by Nasser appeared, weaving all over the place. It headed straight for the crowd. The people dispersed to let it through, and it vanished up one of the many little streets. As the dancing continued, a man approached Steve Thomas. 'Come with me,' he said, 'your driver's in trouble.' Steve went with the man, but after exploring a number of nearby alleys they could find neither Nasser nor the truck. However, a few moments later Nasser appeared some distance away, staggering as though dazed and with blood running from above his eye. Before we could approach him, he had managed to stop a passing taxi and had disappeared in the direction of the government compound. A second man approached Steve and said that Nasser had had a crash. While Steve went to look for the Chevrolet, Ahmed took Michael in his car to the hospital, where we thought Nasser must have gone. However, there was no sign of him. The staff said he had come in but had run out through the back. Eventually Ahmed and Michael found him lying semi-conscious on his bed in the government compound. There was the unmistakable smell of drink. Recognizing Ahmed, Nasser tried to stand up but immediately slumped on to the floor. Ahmed tried to find out what had happened, but Nasser seemed incapable of answering any questions, mumbling at intervals, with a benign smile, 'Sidiki, sidiki' ('My friend, my friend').

Eventually they managed to get the car key from him and went back into the town to see what had happened. The Chevrolet was found at the end of a maze of alleys so narrow that only a drunken man could have got into them with a vehicle that size. Around it was an angry mob. Steve and one of the other drivers, Abdullah, were keeping them at bay. Michael was frightened that perhaps Nasser had killed or injured one of the many little children who play all round the narrow streets, but Ahmed said that it could not be so – if he had, the mob would have manhandled him severely. But the crowd wanted to know where Nasser had got the alcohol. He had damaged the walls of a number of the houses, and he was our driver; they blamed us. However, seeing Ahmed, the crowd calmed down, and after expressing our regrets, we were able to drive away.

That might have been the end of the incident, except that that evening another of our drivers, Salah, also came back into the compound drunk. They were obviously getting alcohol from somewhere, though not from us. However, we did not feel that what a driver did in his spare time was our concern, even though drinking alcohol is against the law for an Omani.

Sur is famous for its singers, and that evening Ahmed took us to a village where we could hear a concert. It was a romantic scene: a crowd of people sitting in the lane between two houses and a group of singers and dancers performing to the accompaniment of elaborate stringed instruments and lit only by two paraffin lamps. The concert had been in progress for perhaps an hour when Salah appeared and said there was more trouble in the compound: Nasser was wandering around half-naked, banging on the doors of all the bungalows and frightening the women, including Ahmed's wife. He said that two of the teachers had overpowered him, but we'd better come and see what was happening for ourselves. Ahmed turned to Michael and said, 'Now will you give him his punishment? Will you let me send him to the Wali?' Michael replied, 'Of course you may send him to the Wali. I don't care if I never see him again.' Ahmed and Salah themselves took Nasser to the Wali, and he was thrown into a cell for the night.

Next morning, Steve and Michael called on the Wali to apologize for the trouble he had been put to. The Wali seemed not at all put out, and only asked what they wanted done with Nasser. They replied that the Wali must do as he thought best, and the Wali said that he would rather Nasser was taken back to Muscat to be dealt with there. We were not due to leave until the next morning, and so the Wali said he would

Old fisherman, Sur.

Madman, Sur.

Traditional dance, Sur.

keep him in the fort until then. Just as Michael and Steve were leaving, the Wali asked if they wanted Nasser fed – which seemed rather a surprising question. 'Of course,' they said, 'he is having a bad enough time as it is, there's no need to starve him as well.' The Wali said that in that case we must bring some food in for him. It began to become clear that, while Nasser worked for us, he was part of our household: we were still responsible for what happened to him, even though he had broken the law.

After leaving the Wali, Steve and Michael went to see the English commander of the local gendarmerie to ask his advice. He looked the part of an English officer: round, red-faced and sweating. He had been very helpful in providing our vehicles with fuel and allowing us to use his radio to send messages back to Muscat. He knew the country well, and we felt sure that he would be able to tell us if we had handled the affair of Nasser correctly. He said so far so good, but there was still a chance that things could turn ugly. There was bound to be some suspicion that we had supplied the drink, and that it could lead to serious trouble. For driving while drunk, Nasser was liable to a punishment which could include being lashed every day for a week. If it was decided that we were to blame for his state, we might receive a similar punishment ourselves. He went on to say that on no account should we attempt to drive back to Muscat with Nasser unless he was in chains and accompanied by an armed escort, otherwise the other drivers might gang together and stage a breakdown to help Nasser to escape and we would be blamed for allowing him to get away. At that point he called in his sergeant and told him to have two armed men equipped with handcuffs to report to us outside the Wali's fort at seven the next morning.

We were already feeling very sorry for Nasser and were beginning to regret that we had allowed him to be handed over to the Wali at all. Our feeling of pity was increased when Steve took Nasser his food. He found a pathetic little figure with two black eyes and a cut on his forehead, crouched in a corner of his dungeon. When Steve entered, he climbed uncertainly to his feet and greeted him with a pathetic cry of '*Sidiki!*'

Next morning, outside the fort, the two armed troopers were waiting for us. The Wali appeared, with the Qadi and his Askars, and led the way into the gatehouse, indicating that we should sit next to him. He ordered the prisoner to be brought before him. The ledge on either side of the gatehouse was lined with white-robed men, many carrying rifles. There were six of us Europeans, Steve and Michael on one side by the Wali and the rest on the ledge opposite. Our two remaining drivers, Salah and Abdullah, with Ferdinand the cook, were sitting directly opposite the Wali. Two of the teachers, a Palestinian and a Jordanian, were summoned so that they could give evidence and translate anything we might not understand. Nasser was brought in and made to stand between two men in the arch that gave on to the courtyard of the fort. He was barefoot and wearing a dirty brown *dishdasha*. While everyone else sat in the shade, a shaft of sunlight bathed him in a golden glow, a theatrical effect.

The Wali asked the prisoner what he had to say for himself, and Nasser launched into his speech. He pleaded; he wrung his hands; he knelt at the Wali's feet; he even wept. Yet for all its theatricality the performance had the ring of truth. He claimed that it was all Salah's fault; that Salah had got him drunk; that he had taken him to a house in Sur where there was an illegal distillery making palm brandy; and that there a group of Salah's friends had held him down and forced him to drink alcohol against his will. Then they had sexually assaulted him. This claim, of course, was greeted with laughter by Salah, who turned to the other people in the court and invited them to share the joke. The Qadi and the Sheikhs joined in the laughter; only the Wali seemed in doubt. Nasser went on to claim that Salah had been against him from the start, and that when he, Nasser, had arrived late on the morning of our departure from Muscat, Salah had threatened to take it out on him. Was this the cause of the quarrel before our departure? We also remembered that on the night of Nasser's crash, Salah had come home drunk as well. While we were debating whether to give this information to the Wali, the Qadi asked Nasser who had blacked his eyes. Nasser said that Salah and his friends had done it. Salah poured scorn on the idea, saying that the Jordanian and Palestinian teachers had done it because Nasser had been frightening the women in the compound. The two teachers turned on Salah and

OMANI GUNBOAT PATROLLING THE STRAITS OF MUSANDAM

RUWI HIGHWAY, NEAR MUTTRAH

DHOW-BUILDING, SUR

DHOW-BUILDING, SUR

DHOW IN THE PORT AT MUTTRAH

OLD DHOWS, SUR

JALALI FORT, MUSCAT

accused him of lying; they said that Nasser already looked as if he had been beaten up when they first saw him. Steve and Michael decided to tell the Wali about Salah's drunkenness, the argument, and our impression that Nasser was the more honest of the two men.

The Wali determined that the only way to check Nasser's story would be to send him with an Askar to see if he could find the house where he claimed that the drink had been forced on him. The half-hour we sat in the gatehouse waiting for their return was very tense. Had we been right to become involved? If the house didn't exist or Nasser couldn't find it, Salah was quite likely to try and get his own back on us by claiming that we had been responsible for providing the alcohol.

In the town, Nasser led the party straight to a house close to where the Chevrolet had been found. The man who owned the house had vanished, but the remains of a pot-still were found.

With this evidence to corroborate Nasser's story, the Wali decided to suspend judgement and send us back to Muscat with both Salah and Nasser. He would send a report to the Wali there. When our two troopers asked if they must handcuff Nasser, the Wali said it wasn't necessary. But he said that they must still accompany us and that one of his Askars must come along as well. Salah would be allowed to drive his Land Rover, but Nasser must not drive the Chevrolet.

By the time we left the fort, the morning was well advanced, and we could not afford anything going wrong if we were to reach Muscat that night. We had only two of our proper drivers, and no one but Steve spoke both English

and Arabic. Bearing in mind the reputation of the tribes, and what the gendarmerie officer had said about staged breakdowns, it was difficult to know whether to set out at all. Yet we had to get back to Muscat to complete our filming schedule and delay would do us no good. We set off, Michael in the first Land Rover, driven by Abdullah, with Nasser and the two army escorts, Salah at the wheel of the second Land Rover with two of our crew, and Bob McShane with Peter and the Askar in the third Land Rover. Steve was driving the Chevrolet with Ferdinand the cook.

An hour out of Sur, at the foot of the first mountain pass, our convoy was stopped by an army road-block. We were surrounded by men with machine-guns, not one of whom spoke English. They looked like asking us to unload every single piece of equipment, and we might be there for hours. The thing we most dreaded was that we might have to pitch camp for the night in unknown country with drivers who might by now be very angry. Salah kept pointing at Steve; it seemed that he was trying to convince the soldiers that Steve had no driving licence and should be sent back to Sur. However, Steve managed to explain who we were. Then Michael showed the officer in charge the Foreign Minister's identification document. That seemed to clinch it. We were allowed to pass.

We drove on over the mountain pass, past the Wahiba Sands, and reached Ebra. Still the expected breakdown had not come. We called at the hospital and picked up our missing driver, Ahmed. He had had a bout of malaria, but was now well enough to drive. We dared not risk stopping for a meal, and pressed on towards Muscat. If we could get as far as the army camp at Bid Bid, we would be safe. There we could find help in the event of trouble, and beyond that the road was passable even at night.

We were just half an hour short of Bid Bid, and it was almost four in the afternoon, when Abdullah stopped his Land Rover without warning. Everyone came to a halt. He said he was worried that it was overheating. He opened the bonnet, while we waited nervously, and eventually seemed content to drive on. But by then we had been going for more than six hours and we agreed to a short break for a drink. Twenty minutes later Michael ordered the restart. To our relief all the drivers climbed back into their vehicles and we drove on.

We reached Muscat before night fell and handed over both our prisoners. We were later told that Salah and Nasser had both been put in Fort Jalali and had lost their jobs. But the authorities seem to have been merciful: less than three weeks later we saw Salah at the wheel of a large official car.

The Interior

A mountain village in the Jebel Akhdar.

At the northern end of the Ruwi valley, where Ruwi stands as the new administrative capital, the road turns into the mountains and winds past the television station towards the airport and the Batinah Coast. This is the road to the Interior, the Oman proper of the days when the country was called Muscat and Oman. Many people still talk of 'travelling to the Oman' when they mean they are driving an hour out of Muscat. There is a fundamental difference between the inhabitants of the Interior and the people of the coast, which helps to explain much of the conflict that has always seemed to exist between them. The coast-dwellers, being fishermen and sailors, travelling abroad and meeting outsiders, have always been more outward-looking and more ready to accept change than the ultra-conservative men of the Interior. Deeply religious, the inland dwellers belong to a puritanical Moslem sect, the Ibadhis, who preach a return to the original principles of Islam. Ibadhism was forcibly expunged from the rest of Arabia, but took root in the mountains of Oman, where it remains today. Ibadhism does not believe in outward show, and until very recently continued to call upon its adherents to slay all unbelievers, which could have meant other Moslems who did not agree with them as much as infidels.

Officially, the Interior used to begin where the Ruwi hospital now stands by the side of the main road. There, overlooked by a watchtower perched high on an inaccessible crag, stands a forlorn mud hut. This was Said bin Taimur's customs post in the days when he imposed an arbitrary duty on all goods 'imported' into the capital area, and where he attempted to effect some measure of control over the inhabitants by increasing the rates if they were growing restive (for without the markets of Muttrah and Muscat, a farmer in the Interior would stand little chance of making a living), and by preventing the traffic of arms. This customs post now stands sadly neglected and empty, bypassed by the new tarmac road. The internal customs may have departed with the old Sultan, but his incomprehensible method of calculating duty still remains. When we went to the airport to collect some replacement equipment for the film, the customs officer added in the date before working out the amount he wanted. We had already been waiting over an hour, so we paid up without arguing.

Our first visit to the Interior together was a day trip to Bahla before the rest of the crew arrived. It is a journey for which foreigners still require a permit, as it is reputed to be somewhat hazardous. Since Richard's initial meeting with Sayyed Fahar, we had planes to fly us on advance trips to the towns and villages in which we wanted to film so that we could sort out with everyone concerned when we would be back with the camera. We had to go in person since there are as yet no postal services to the Interior and no telephones outside the capital area.

We flew west from Seeb over the most incredible terrain, an artist's wild impression of a moonscape. It looked an ideal training ground for astronauts. As the sun hit the rocks at different angles, the colours changed every yard through various shades of red and brown. The rocks were tortured and twisted, and from the air we could see every fault and fold, like illustrations in an elementary geography book. Most of the rocks were forced up through the limestone of the main mountain chain when Arabia emerged from the sea millions of years ago. It is reputed to

Potter, Bahla.

be the largest surface deposit on earth of igneous rock from deep down in the crust.

We flew down the Wadi Sumail, one of the three passable gaps in the massive mountainous backbone of northern Oman. On our left the moonscape stretched away into the heat haze; on our right, like a wall, towered the bulk of the impenetrable Jebal Akhdar, the Green Mountain. On top of the Jebal is a wild plateau, dissected by years of earthquake, sun and rain into deep fissures and tortured ravines. Because of its height, the plateau enjoys more rain than most parts of Oman, and it has even been known to snow there. Among the bare rocks is a remarkable valley, where half a dozen tiny villages, chief of which is Sayq, cling to the cliff. The face of the mountain has been carved into terraces where there are orchards of pomegranates, peaches, figs, apricots and vines. Walnut trees and roses bloom in the carefully tended gardens. Legends tell of leopards roaming up there, and of a great snake, embossed like a shield. Impossible to reach except by foot, donkey or plane, the fertile valley which gives the Green Mountain its name is only one small oasis in a mass of bare stone.

Beneath us, as we flew down the Wadi Sumail, every so often we would see a khaki patch in the distance: an oasis, with its dusty date palms under which an entire community lived. Leading to each of them was a strange line of equidistant circles, like the spoil from the tunnelling of a giant mole. We discovered that they were indeed heaps of spoil, from the *falaj*. The *falaj* is almost a symbol of Oman. It is certainly the most important item of her heritage, for it is the means by which the towns and villages obtain their water. The *falaj* system of irrigation was introduced to Oman by the Persians more than 2,000 years ago. A water source, which may be a spring or the natural water-table, is located in the mountains and the water is led down to the area that needs it by means of an underground channel – built by sinking vertical shafts at intervals of between twenty and fifty yards and connecting the bottoms. The water emerges above the village into a stone channel. Where it has to cross a *wadi*, it does so by means of a U-bend, an inverted syphon. The water for drinking is drawn at the top of the village. Further down

Potter, Bahla.

Water pots, Bahla.

the channel places are reserved for bathing and for washing dishes before the water is led on into the date gardens. Once in the gardens, the water is led round and round, while individual garden owners take turns to channel it into their own plot. Each person is allowed half an hour at a time, and if he goes over, must pay a fine to the man following whose water he has taken. At Rostaq we saw a large sundial, some twenty yards by six, from which is calculated the time a man can have water. Since the water

never completely stops running, even in times of severe drought, the date gardens are watered night and day. (During the night the position of the moon and stars is used to calculate time.) *Falaj* irrigation is often supplemented by artesian wells. Oman is more fortunate with its water supply than most of Arabia, but water is still a precious commodity.

We landed at Nizwa, a former capital of the Interior and centre of the Imamate wars of the 1950s; it is where the rebel Imam used to live. There are two airstrips at Nizwa. One, alongside the army camp, runs straight into an 800-foot wall of rock. Fortunately we landed at the other, the Firq strip, around the corner of the mountain but sited on the plain. As we made our descent, we saw the shell of an old plane which had crashed in 1958. Our pilot made a perfect landing, shingle streaming out from behind the wheels. Half a dozen soldiers were there to meet us, sheltering from the sun in a hut the size of a bus shelter, next to which was a barbed-wire compound of fuel drums. It had been arranged in Muscat that we would have an army driver to meet us and take us on to Bahla, an hour's ride away over rough roads. There was a Land Rover by the hut, but we were assured it was not for us. A sergeant called up the Nizwa camp on his radio to obtain some transport to get us as far as the mess. Firq, four miles down the road from Nizwa, is a small town where indigo is grown. Dyeing is its most important industry, and along the banks of its *falaj* men and women can be seen filling enormous pots with indigo and water.

The mess at Nizwa is a colonial-style building which would need no alteration for use as a film set: whitewashed brick walls, a roof made from black-painted poles covered with

Potter's kiln, Bahla.

palm-frond matting, a lazy fan circulating still warm air. We explained our predicament to the duty officer, who said that although he was short of transport he would see what he could do. While we were waiting, we consumed *loomies*, a soft drink made from fresh limes which we were informed was typically Omani, but which turned out to be typical only of the British officers. After an hour the duty officer returned with a Land Rover and we set out for Bahla. Only when we returned to Nizwa that evening did we learn that our driver had been at the airstrip all the time and had even asked one of us for a match. It transpired that although he had been briefed in three languages – English, Arabic and Hindi – his instructions had been to go to Firq and collect the television. Since no set had come off our plane he had stayed put!

We drove through the centre of Nizwa past the circular tower fort which dominates the town. Just over 100 feet high and solid stone for most of its height, its diameter is 150 feet. It was built in the seventeenth century by the local Imam as a defence against the Portuguese. In the twelve years it took to complete, you might think the Portuguese would have overrun the entire country; but it was, in fact, that same Imam, Sultan bin Said, who finally ejected them from Muscat and Oman. Unwanted prisoners were thrown from its roof, a practice which is rumoured to have continued into Said bin Taimur's reign. During the Imamate war, Nizwa was besieged by British Indian troops. The brigadier in charge had run low on ammunition for his ancient screw guns. When he signalled back for more, his commander was heard to say, 'Good God, Corky, go easy with that ammo. That's the last like that outside the Poona

Museum!' The RAF was ordered up to bomb the fort instead, only to see its rockets bounce off the walls: the marks can be seen today.

Nizwa is famed for its dates and its halwa, which we saw being stirred in large vats over wood fires. Also in the *Souk* can be found silversmiths and coppersmiths working on elaborate khunjars, coffee-pots and jewellery. Nizwa has been an acknowledged centre of metal-crafts since ancient times, when copper was mined in Oman. The present lack of local copper does not worry the craftsmen, as an official handout explained: 'Today's craftsmen in Nizwa can be seen making use of a ready-made supply of copper from the radiators of wrecked vehicles. Both motoring and cars have a short history in Oman, travelling conditions and the inexperience of drivers ensuring a fairly steady supply of copper.'

We decided not to film at Nizwa, even though it has such a large and busy *Souk*, because in terms of development it is a half-way town. The main road is tarmac and the outskirts are full of modern buildings, including a hospital built and opened within an impressive seventy-two days. Its importance as a regional centre seems to have deprived it of some of that tribal identity which lingers in other, smaller towns.

We went therefore to Bahla, another former capital of the Interior. It is a large oasis in a cradle of hills, watched over by an impressive seventeenth-century mud fort. From its massive but now crumbling ramparts hung a limp Omani flag. Around the entire perimeter of the town runs a mud-brick wall, twelve miles long, the largest and longest in Oman, once guarded by a special detachment of slaves. Apart from a few modern buildings, the entire town, including the

Water sundial: each stone represents a member of the village, and when the shadow falls on a stone it gives the family fifteen minutes of water to irrigate their fields.

date gardens and wheatfields, is contained inside the fortifications.

We went to the fort, to meet the Wali and obtain his permission to look around. The Ministry of the Interior had promised to send a radio message to warn him of our arrival; each Wali, and there are thirty-seven at the moment, is issued with a radio set and given a time at which to make daily contact with Muscat. But he was nowhere to be seen. As we were leaving the fort to try his official residence, a new cement-block bungalow a mile out of town, a Land Rover, with an open back overflowing with gun-toting guards, screeched to a halt. The guards toppled out as the Wali, a short man with buck teeth and a wispy black beard, climbed from the driving seat. In the cab sat his son, a miniature replica of his father without the beard, roaring with laughter. We were to discover that his father's driving always sent him into paroxysms of mirth. When we were filming at Al Ghafat, the Wali turned up unexpectedly (Al Ghafat being in his territory), his car lurching through the village in kangaroo-like hops, his son still by his side laughing. When the time came for him to leave, and we were filming his departure, he

Young boy writing a letter for his father, Rostaq.

climbed stiffly into the passenger seat and allowed one of his guards to drive.

It was only while we were having coffee with the Wali that the message arrived from Muscat to announce our visit. With permission granted to see the town, the Wali gave us one of his Askars to accompany us. Bahla is famous for pottery, and we went to the potters' quarter. Craftsmen's skills are handed down from father to son, and the way in which the Bahla potters work, turning their wheels with their feet, produces pottery identical to examples of pre-Islamic work discovered by archaeologists. Outside the house in which Saif bin Amor and his son Said were working lay clay in pits. Inside, the old man was making incense burners while his son was producing water-jars. He can throw fifty a day. In one corner of the crowded room stood larger jars, like Ali Baba baskets, lengths of rope wound round the outsides to prevent the jars collapsing before firing. These are used to store dates. Next to the clay-pits outside were the kilns, like ten-foot beehives, into which the finished articles were carefully placed. Once the kilns are full, the door is sealed and a fire is lit underneath, a process which happens approximately every three months. The finished pots are loaded on to donkeys ready for the long arduous journey to the *Souk* at Muscat or Muttrah. The journey takes a week or more, and many pots are broken on the way. No wonder the potters seem to be philosophers!

Bahla Health Centre is a new building under the shadow of the old fort. It has only twenty-four beds, but deals with upwards of 400 out-patients a day. Despite the truly heroic efforts of the doctors and nurses here and elsewhere, Oman still has a long way to go in its fight

Medical Officer for the Bahla Health Centre.

against disease. Things are already far better than they once were, but sadly trachoma is still prevalent, and children are still known in some parts to die from malaria. But not all those who make their way to the health centre in the morning are in desperate need of medicine. The hospitals, health centres and clinics have brought another great social change to Oman. Previously women would leave their homes only to go to the well or *falaj* to draw water, dressed in black if there was any chance of a stranger seeing them. Women still do not do the shopping.

Bedouin women, Bahla Health Centre.

The men buy all the food, and even the women's clothes. Now, however, in the more enlightened atmosphere it is socially acceptable for women to visit the hospital, either with their children or alone, and many of the daily out-patients are there to meet friends and have a chat.

At four o'clock, when the town had awakened from its siesta, the *Souk* reopened. Like most *Souks*, the one in Bahla is built around a square from which run a warren of covered alleyways. In an open space on the edge of the *Souk*, a man wandered slowly round in circles talking to himself. His legs were shackled, and the clinking of his chains mingled with the cries of men selling dates, apricots and goats. He was mad and he was shackled to prevent him from running off or becoming violent. He was fed and cared for by the villagers. Nearby, camels and donkeys were tethered to a tree. The camel was once the chief means of transport in Oman, but it has now been superseded by the Land Rover, whereas the main work animal is the donkey. A public scribe sat on the ground, pen in hand, paper on knee, composing a letter for an illiterate customer.

We went to watch a weaver at work beneath the grey crumbling wall of the fort. He sat in a shallow pit, under a frond awning, in front of his loom. The coarse strands of goat-wool ran out into the sunlight to be anchored to the ground a few yards away. As he talked to us, his busy hands threw the bobbin backwards and forwards. He told us he was 140 years old. Omanis have little exact feeling for time. Every generation is considered to be approximately twenty years, and he was calculating his age by the generations he had seen and begotten. He was probably in his eighties.

Most Omanis wear a watch; but ask a man the time and he will study his wrist, then look up at the sun before giving an answer. To confuse the unwary visitor even more, the time of day is reckoned from 5 p.m., so that Moslem time is seven hours in advance of standard time.

The weaver claimed that his longevity was due to the four kilos of dates he used to eat every day – a quantity that grew from one kilo as he realized that we were listening appreciatively – and the daily litre of honey that he drank. He told us, with relish, how he had been a sailor in the Gulf before returning to Bahla to take over weaving from his father. He was saddened that his oldest boy did not want to enter the trade and had opted for an office job in Muscat. When he had had enough of spinning his tales, he tottered off up the hill to the mosque for his late-afternoon prayers.

Bahla has an unenviable reputation for being the centre of witchcraft, the home of the *djinn* and a place where black magic is practised. The *djinn* are devils which lead men astray, and they are supposed to live on a white mountain a mile or two from the town. This mountain is an 'exotic'; that is, geologically, it ought not to be there. Oman has the largest collection of exotics in the world; it is thought that they were deposits brought by the sea from Iran and left behind when the land was formed. It is easy to see why the witch mountain has caught the imagination, as it gleams white in the sunlight, a strange contrast to the greys, blacks and reds of the surrounding hills. Omanis from other parts of the country say the wall around Bahla was built to keep in the *djinn* (Bahla inhabitants claim it is to keep them out), and they tread warily if made to enter the town. They talk in whispers of people who travelled to Bahla never to be seen again in human form.

When we came back to Bahla to film, escorted this time by an Omani army officer, we camped near the village of Jabrin, two miles down the road, half-way to Al Ghafat, another village where we wanted to work. Our first day of filming in Bahla was chaotic. The Wali knew we were coming, but he had unfortunately forgotten to tell anybody else. The weaver had dismantled his loom to rebuild it, and the potters had gone to Muscat. It was all very frustrating. When a whirlwind swept through our camp site that evening, lifting paper, bushes and cans fifty feet into the air, the drivers huddled together saying, 'It is the *djinn*, sent from Bahla because you have annoyed them.' We half believed them. Jabrin is another town with a fort, possibly the most impressive in Oman. Built as a country retreat for the Imams of the seventeenth century, its distinction and pride are the beautiful painted ceilings now being carefully restored. Jabrin itself is a tiny oasis which lies away from the Jebal Akhdar, on the edge of the gravel plains. Its people grow tomatoes, dates and grapes. The main square of the village has an open *majlis*, where the townspeople gather under an old tamarind tree. Nearby were tethered two very fine-looking horses. Once Oman was famed for its Arab stallions, but no longer. The only horses we saw in all Oman were at Jabrin.

Our camp site was near the top of the Jabrin *falaj*. We camped around a thorn tree, put up tents for the equipment and dug a hole near to the cook's tent for his rubbish; this became a paradise for the goats of the nomad Bedou, which would eat anything going, especially cardboard boxes. Some of us slept

Young boy in the fort at Rostaq.

in the tents, others in the open, but we all had mosquito nets. Being close to water, as soon as you lay down you would hear a steady drone and would lie there wondering where it was, and whether you could kill it before it got you. Our Omani officer had said to us the first night as we set up our nets, 'Oh, you won't need those.' The next morning he came to us covered in bites and said, 'Please, have you a spare net for me?' The nets also kept out the scorpions and camel spiders.

When we were in Muscat everybody had

THE OLD FORT, SUR

HOT SPRINGS, ROSTAQ

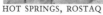

VIEW FROM THE OLD FORT, ROSTAQ

DOMESTIC SCENE, MUTTRAH

FARMWORKERS, IN THE INTERIOR

MUSCAT

THE KORAN AND KHUNJAR

KORANIC SCHOOL, ROSTAQ

CARVED DOOR, MUSCAT

SCHOOLTEACHER, BAHLA

DIRECTOR OF EDUCATION FOR THE SUR REGION, AHMED GHAZALI

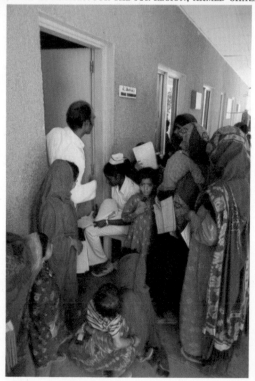

HEALTH CENTRE, BAHLA

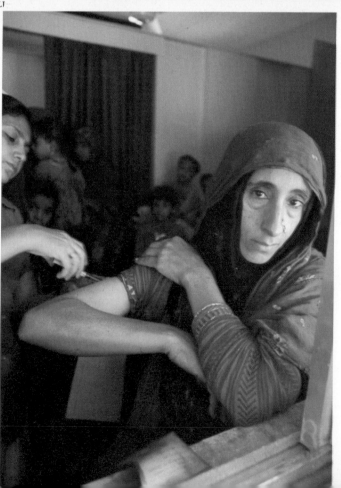

BEDOUIN WOMEN, HEALTH CENTRE, BAHLA

A VIEW OF AL GHAFAT

VIEW THROUGH THE GATES OF ROSTAQ FORT

OLD SILVERSMITH, SUR

WATER POTS, BAHLA

Farmworkers, Bahla.

Adviser to the Wali of Rostaq.

told us about these giant spiders; but we were comforted by the thought that those who really knew the Interior said we would never actually see them. With one month's experience, during which time we had seen nothing frightening, we were scornful of such stories, and we all joked a lot about creepy-crawlies.

On our first night in Jabrin we had finished our meal and were sitting round (we carried chairs with us) drinking a cup of tea by starlight; one of the great glories of Arabia is the clarity of the sky at night, so close you feel you can touch the stars. We had not bothered to light the oil lamps, but sat, dim silhouettes, talking. Suddenly Michael jumped in the air with a cry of alarm. Something had walked across his bare foot and started to climb his leg. We leapt to our feet, knocking chairs over in our hurry, and switched on our torches. There, moving at high speed towards the tents, was this Thing, our first camel spider. It is called a camel spider because the scorpion climbs on its back and rides several miles. Only when British soldiers used to put them in a biscuit tin and shake them up did the camel spider and scorpion fight; every time the spider won. It doesn't look like a spider. It has eight legs, of course, but it has a huge, grotesque abdomen and a large round head and looks more like a giant wasp. On the front of its head are a couple of wicked-looking pincers, and if one nips you, you know all about it for twenty-four hours. It is about four or five inches across.

Every night at Jabrin we would kill at least half a dozen of these creatures inside the tents, which was not easy since they move fast. We were also plagued with scorpions. We had to be very careful in the morning to shake out clothes and shoes to make sure none had climbed in

Weaver, Bahla.

during the night. We were all jumpy about scorpions, particularly Bob, the assistant camera-man. The night we camped at Rostaq on the other side of the mountain, he had gone to take a shower in the nearby army camp. With glee the following morning our Omani officer appeared at breakfast with a tin and said, 'Look what I found in the shower after Bob had left.' And on to the ground he tossed a dead scorpion. Bob paled. It was the first time he had actually seen one. At last he said, 'It's not as big as I

Koranic School, Rostaq.

Koranic School, Rostaq.

Koranic School, Rostaq.

thought,' but added a few minutes later, in an earnest voice, 'Do you know, those scorpions are so small, we're going to have to be extra careful from now on.' As we finished breakfast Bob suddenly shouted, 'A giant scorpion!' 'Where?' we cried, jumping up. He picked up a mallet, and ran across the stones. We followed, rather nervous since none of us could see it. There, blowing in the breeze, was an apple wrapper.

The nastiest incident involved one of our drivers. The film crew slept on camp beds; the drivers and soldiers just put down a bedroll on the ground. One evening, when we were sipping our bedtime tea, there was a disturbance among the drivers. We went over to find out what was happening. One of the drivers had been sleeping on his back and had woken to the feel of something on his chest. Fortunately, he hadn't moved. He opened his eyes to find himself face to face with a puff-adder. This is a very slow-moving snake, which is what makes it so dangerous. Unlike most snakes, it does not get out of the way of humans, so people can walk very close to it. Then it has one of the fastest strikes of any snake. The driver managed to throw it off himself. None of the crew would sleep that night.

About half an hour to the west of our camp, nestling in the lee of a 5,000-foot shoulder of bare rock, was Al Ghafat. A straight track points like a finger at the spot where the village shelters in a cluster of palms. Entering the oasis, one is struck not only by the coolness but by the beauty of the village, surely one of the cleanest and most perfect in all Oman. There are no rusty tin cans or scraps of paper lying at the side of the road. Getting out of a vehicle in the middle

Shepherd in the Interior.

of the village one notices the quiet. There is an immediate feeling of order. Not only are all the white baked-clay houses in good repair; there are no out-of-place bits of cement block or garish plastic and metal fittings.

Al Ghafat is the home of the Beni Hina tribe, strict members of the Ibadhi sect. Sheikh Abdullah is the head of the tribe. It was Malcolm Dennison who first took Michael there. He warned Michael that he should not worry if Sheikh Abdullah at first seemed rather aloof –

until a few years ago his religious scruples would have prevented him from sitting in the same room as a Christian at all. The Sheikh has a reputation for being alarmingly well informed. Visitors are advised to catch up on world news before calling on him, as he is likely to ask a series of sharp and knowledgeable questions about anything from the latest moonshot to student unrest in Europe. He is a bright-eyed, hook-nosed, wizened man, with a spectacularly pierced ear. He greeted Michael and Malcolm warmly and led them upstairs to his *majlis*. It was a simple but astonishingly beautiful room, fifteen feet long and ten feet wide, with a low plain beamed ceiling. Its appeal lay in its perfect proportions and the muted browns, greys and dun colours of its bare beams and dry clay and straw walls. The total effect was of cool and repose. Through deeply recessed windows, one looked out to the limpid green palm trees and felt protected from the glaring sunlight reflected off the village houses and the harsh mountainside. Below was a *falaj* where a girl in the brightest coloured robes was washing her hair. The only sounds were the distant chatter of women, running water in the *falaj* and the occasional bleat of goats.

After coffee, Sheikh Abdullah's eldest son, Sheikh Mohammed, offered to show Michael round the village. Abdullah is the Sheikh of the tribe, but each of his sons is given the title of Sheikh and treated with deference by the people of the villages. Sheikh Mohammed is a tall, straight young man in his twenties, with a handsome black beard, who runs a family construction business and speaks very good English. Sheikh Abdullah's family is one of the most influential in Oman. Many of his relatives are successful businessmen and big landowners.

His younger brother is the Sultan's Minister of Islamic Affairs.

Al Ghafat has a population of about 2,000. Many of the men work for the Sheikh. Instead of wages, the Sheikh gives them palms and land so that they can make their own living and grow their own food. Others own land and trees in their own right, but there is not enough land or work to support everyone, so many men have to seek work outside the village. Some go to Muscat, to work in jobs connected with development, while others drive over to neighbouring Dubai and Abu Dhabi. According to the *Book of the Prophet Suleiman*, Al Ghafat once had 1,000 wells; now there are barely 300, so the villagers are confident that they can dig many more. Mohammed showed Michael a spot where two men were digging at the bottom of a fifty-foot shaft. Before starting work, they had sought the advice of a local wise man about where to dig. After consulting the *Book of the Prophet Suleiman* he had chosen this spot. They had been digging for six weeks, and sure enough, they had just struck water. In many villages the continual hunt for new sources of water has damaged the supply they already have. The indiscriminate sinking of wells and motorized pumping of water has lowered the water-table all round. Even Sheikh Mohammed, who is well versed in modern engineering principles, feigned ignorance of the effects of lowering the water-table. When a neighbour accused him of reducing the amount of water in his well by sinking a new one of his own only a few yards away and pumping off water to irrigate a new field, he retorted: 'What's he complaining about? The new well is on my ground, not his!' Traditionally one of Oman's greatest assets has been water, but with development and industrialization there is now nothing like enough to meet the increasing demand. The Sultan is aware that he needs a coordinated policy for water conservation run by a central body with overriding control. But first he will have to convince the traditional owners of the waters that it is in the nation's best interest to share what they once monopolized. It may prove problematic, but Qaboos is noted for his persuasive powers.

Al Ghafat stands 1,000 feet above sea-level. With its good water supply, it is one of the best agricultural areas in the country. In a good year its fields can produce as many as three crops of wheat; this in spite of the fact that the implements are identical to those used centuries ago. There are no tractors, and the only ploughs are single-bladed and made of wood, drawn by oxen. The fields also produce good crops of onions, melons and lucerne (for cattle feed). As well as date palms, there are oranges, limes and bananas. Although only about 150 square miles of the whole of Oman are under cultivation, about 80 per cent of the population is still engaged in agriculture. Until the discovery of oil, dates were the country's principal export. Now there are ambitious plans to use the oil revenue to improve agriculture, in the hope that Oman may one day become one of the principal food producers of the Arab world. Already tobacco and sugarcane are being exported.

After his initial visit, and comparing it with other villages in the Interior, Michael decided to feature Al Ghafat in the film. However, as far as we could discover, no one had filmed or photographed it before, and we were not at all sure that Sheikh Abdullah, with his strict religious views, would agree to our bringing a camera to his village. It was decided that the only thing to do was for Michael to return with Malcolm Dennison's Omani assistant, Mahmoud, and see if he could persuade Sheikh Abdullah to agree. There was no way in which we could warn him of the visit in advance – there are, of course, no telephones, and the Sheikh has no radio – so Michael and Mahmoud persuaded the air force to fly them up from Muscat by helicopter. As they circled to find a suitable spot to land outside the village, the noise of the rotor attracted a large crowd of excited villagers. Hardly had they landed when Sheikh Abdullah arrived in his Land Rover to see what was going on. It was a touching sight. As the old man walked into the middle of his people, many took their sandals off as a mark of respect. He seemed a bit surprised at Michael and Mahmoud's noisy entrance, but was probably also a little flattered that they had made a special journey in a helicopter just to see him. At any event, he welcomed them like old friends.

In Sheikh Abdullah's *majlis* the conversation was slowly turned towards the purpose of the visit. The Sheikh was told that we were making a film about the whole of Oman, and we hoped that when people in England saw the film they would feel sympathy for the people of Oman. Suddenly the old man put his head on one side and asked, 'Why are you British suddenly so interested in Oman? For all those years under Said bin Taimur you ignored us. Could it be that you are now interested in our oil?' Michael had to confess that he might be right. Sheikh Abdullah chuckled and led the conversation into a survey of world politics. When at length Michael was able to pop the question and ask if he would let us come and film in his village, he beamed delightedly. 'Of course,' he said, 'you are most welcome, but I have agreed only because you have been so polite.' Then he led Michael and Mahmoud round the village, stopping every so often, outside a house, by the mosque, or near a date garden, to shake his head and say, 'To think all this will be seen in Paris!'

Our actual filming in Al Ghafat was the most pleasant and relaxed work we did anywhere in Oman. The temperature was well over 100°F, but we could always return to the cool of the *majlis*. There we were plied with glasses of cool water and fresh fruit. At mealtimes we were served with the best food in Oman.

Michael's wife Sophie had just flown out from London to join us, and was still suffering particularly badly from the heat. So Sheikh Mohammed suggested that, rather than trailing around all the time with us, she might like to go and sit with the women. She was taken into a sitting-room similar to the men's *majlis*, except that the floor was covered in elaborately embroidered cushions in addition to the Persian carpets. There the women of the Sheikh's family and their friends sat and talked. The children came and went, talked and played, as they chose. Sophie is an educationalist, and what struck her was the relaxed way in which the adults accepted the presence of the children. There were none of the outbursts of adult irritation that you find in Western households when children play in a room where adults are talking. Another thing she noticed was the absence of toys. It is an accepted idea in the West that dolls are a natural and fundamental part of childhood; in Oman none of the girls seemed to have them, nor to crave for them. Their mothering instinct seems in no way impaired.

The women asked Sophie a number of times if she would like to have a swim. She assumed that they either didn't mean it or had got hold of the wrong word. But when they continued to press her, she said that she would. They took her into a secluded courtyard, gave her a towel and told her to take her clothes off. She was shown through a door where there were steps leading down into the ground. At the bottom of the steps she found that the *falaj* ran under the house and there was a stone pool full of fresh clear running water. It was reminiscent of a Roman bath.

We asked Sheikh Mohammed if we too could see the women's *majlis*. 'Of course,' he said, and led us into the room. It was cool, shaded, and completely empty – not a woman in sight! Sophie admired the village so much that Sheikh Mohammed made her a gift of one of the empty houses. So now the Darlows have a get-away cottage, though it is hard to see how they can use it. The return air fare of £450 ($900), and then twelve hours in a Land Rover, is just a bit much for a weekend, though it is one of the most beautiful and romantic houses in the world and complete with an underground bath.

The heat was beginning to get everybody down. Our filming was nearing the finish, and the summer had really started. The temperature stayed in the hundreds even during the coldest part of the night. During the day it was 130°F in the shade. Cans of orange juice bubbled. Canned luncheon meat, which would be swimming with liquid when opened, would dry out so quickly that if it wasn't eaten within five minutes it became rock-hard and inedible. There was no way we could keep anything cool. By seven

Religious leader, Rostaq.

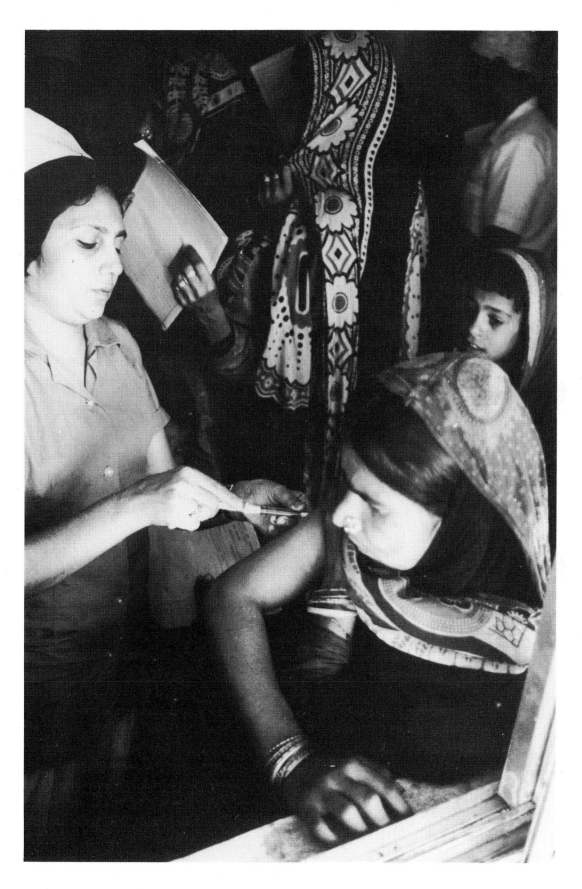

Bedouin woman, Bahla Health Centre.

Rostaq Souk.

o'clock every morning, even if you didn't move, the sweat was pouring off you. One of the more pleasant experiences was to go down to the *falaj*. The channel was about four feet wide and the water six inches deep. In spite of the leeches – and the nibbles of the fish that were there to eat the mosquito larvae – it was heaven to lie in the lukewarm water.

The heat was too much not only for us but for some of our film equipment. The equipment had taken a pounding from travelling more than 3,000 miles on rough roads, and dust had got in everywhere. In spite of having specially insulated boxes for the camera, we found that the camera body reached a temperature of 100°F within a few minutes of being taken from its box and switched on, although it was still protected by a special reflective space blanket. On one occasion we found a sticky deposit in the camera gate: the film had melted.

The motor which synchronized the tape recorder with the camera broke down, and Richard had to return to Muscat for a replacement. We had made arrangements with the air force that our rushes would be flown out from the nearest airstrip every two days, so that we could put them on a plane to London. With no way of keeping the film cool, if we had not got them out the film would have been ruined. Film crews in Arabia have discovered that unopened film stock can expose itself in the can in such heat. It is a tribute to the technical crew, who nursed their equipment like sick babies, that we did not lose a single foot of film because of malfunctioning equipment.

When, at the end of May, we broke camp to return to Muscat, we were not sorry. Our filming was almost over, and not even the charm of the people could make up for the climate of the Interior.

Oil

As one drives west from the mountains, the jagged multicoloured outcrops quickly give way to a stony, undulating plain which stretches as far as the eye can see. Small boulders mark the edge of the road, which is made of earth levelled and packed by a machine like a giant spider with wheels. In 1970, there were only six miles of metalled road in the entire country, all of it at Muscat. Elsewhere the only way to travel was in a Land Rover, picking your way between boulders, or on a camel, or on a donkey: all three slow and tedious methods. There are now more than 4,000 miles of graded roads, many of them forced through the mountains in an impressive feat of engineering, and some 400 miles have been given a tarmac surface.

The road on which we travelled west had been one of the first to be built, by the oil company; it runs from the oilfields of the Interior to the tanker terminal on the coast. There is no vegetation except for a few straggly thorn bushes, and if the wind blows, it curls the plume of dust rising from behind the vehicle, making it look like a crop sprayer. Unsignposted tracks branch off at intervals, seeming to head nowhere, and you are never quite certain that you are still on the right route. Drivers like Malcolm Dennison, experienced in the Interior, often do not use the tracks at all, but navigate by lining themselves up on the mountains as they had to in the old days. One eye is always watching those mountains for the tell-tale clouds that mean a storm. The tracks cross, and sometimes follow, *wadis* – watercourses which do not appear to have seen water for many years. But when it does rain, here or several miles away in the mountains, a wall of water sweeps along the *wadis* carrying everything before it, including vehicles. As

quickly as it came, the water rushes past, out into the desert, leaving the wadi floor dry and cracked again.

Two hours clear of the mountains, like a mirage in the distance, a cluster of buildings appears, dancing in the heat. Out here the stones tremble only a few yards away. Drawing closer, one can see huge flames, like orange beacons, and soon the quiet of the desert is broken by the dull roar of the burning gases. This is Fahud, the heart of the oilfields from which the wealth of the country comes.

Fahud is still in the semi-desert of the gravel plains, which in a few miles become the sands and sweeping dunes of the Rub al Khali, the Empty Quarter of Arabia, where few men venture. The gravel plains may not be T. E. Lawrence's idea of a desert, about which Englishmen tend to become lyrical and romantic; but they are still lonely, forbidding places where the only shade is man-made and no one stays out in the sun unless he has to. We had thought our camp site at Jabrin was hot, but the arid heat of Fahud was unbearable, and we were glad we did not have to stay there long.

It took a long time to discover oil in Oman. The first concessions for exploration were granted to a foreign consortium in 1925, but very little happened until 1937, when the concessions were reallocated. Even then, exploration was curtailed first of all by the Second World War, and then by the tribal wars of the 1950s, during which the Sultan controlled the Interior in name only. Since the Sultan had granted the concessions, an oil man going into the Interior was welcomed with a bullet. Serious exploration did not start until 1956, towards the end of the Imamate war. At first, prospects did not seem hopeful. Searches concentrated on the Fahud area, where there is a fold in the strata that appeared ideal, and similar geological features nearby. At Fahud itself, the Petroleum Development (Oman) Company (PDO), put down a final well and found nothing, and its major shareholders, including British Petroleum, decided to withdraw, leaving Shell to take over the management.

Exploration continued, and in 1962 a small find was made at Yibal, a few miles from Fahud. The following year another discovery was made at Natih, and in 1964 oil was discovered at Fahud. This last find decided PDO to enter commercial production, and in August 1967 oil was first exported from Oman. The Fahud borehole was less than 400 yards from the abortive attempt of the previous consortium. The discovery of oil brought the country's first real revenue since the eighteenth century.

Most visitors now fly into Fahud, landing on the gravel runway, where every day a Skyvan puts in with fresh supplies for the oil camp. When we arrived, we buzzed the camp to alert the firefighting crew and circled a few times to give them time to travel the mile to the airstrip. We landed and walked across to a concrete shelter to await our transport. Inside the shelter were a plastic container of deliciously cold iced water, a rough wooden bench, and heaps of baggage tags under what looked like a never-used schedule board. We were astonished to learn that Fahud is a scheduled airport for some internal flights and even for some to neighbouring Arab countries.

The oil camp gives the impression of having dropped from the sky. A few cement-block bungalows for senior executives sit in a neat row, with views on a clear day across a wide expanse of arid plain to the foothills of the Jebal Akhdar. Rows of air-conditioned trailers for the other employees cluster, as if arranged in a huge open-air showroom. On a small hillock, overlooking the camp, is an outpost of the Oman gendarmerie, there to guard the oil installations, its flag as limp as we felt. A low building carried the impressive sign 'FAHUD HILTON'; it was the bar, frequented by foreigners. Next to it were the canteen, where we had one of our best European-style meals in the whole of Oman, and an open-air cinema.

Standing in the middle of the complex is a gleaming modern pumping station, the hub of the oil system. Here, all oil from the surrounding fields is gathered, after it has been separated from water and gas, and is piped underground the 200 miles to the coast. The gas is burnt off at the moment, although there are plans to utilize it for powering a coastal desalination plant. The water and oil are separated in an enclosed area of pipes, retorts and valves, like a giant's kitchen. The water is brackish and unusable, and is either released into the desert or put back down the wells to help force up the oil. There are no natural sources of fresh water at Fahud, and drinking-water has to be obtained from a plant capable of producing 20,000 gallons a day, using the principle called reverse osmosis.

To the uninitiated, Fahud does not look very much like an oil camp. There are none of those rigs which stand out on the skyline in John Wayne films. The well-heads are simply giant valves, standing a couple of feet out of the ground, each with two pipes in which you can hear the rhythmic heartbeat of the oil.

The pipeline to the coast rises to its highest spot 2,000 feet up in the mountains near Iski, where there is a controlling valve ready for the oil's downward rush to the tank farm, a cluster of silver tanks hidden in the crook of a hill, by the small bay of Mina al Fahal at the southern end of the Batinah Coast, where the mountains of the Interior reach the sea and break the 200-mile stretch of sand. Mina is the Arabic word for a port, and Fahal is a name taken from a barren lump of rock a few hundred yards from the shore. It means 'victory', and was given after the Portuguese destroyed the Turkish fleet there in 1553. In the bay, motionless as cardboard cut-outs, sit tankers of every size waiting their turn to connect to the buoys which load the oil.

The first outcrops overlooking Mina al Fahal are covered with European-style box houses, the first modern housing development in Oman. The centre of social life is the Ras al Hamra Recreation Centre, tucked in to one end of a sandy beach from which people swim, sail and water-ski. The bars and the restaurant, which serves a renowned curry lunch every Friday (the day off in Oman), overlook a salt-water swimming pool. A lifebelt by the side of the pool carries the legend S.S. HARDSHIP, and although the setting may look idyllic, the water is too warm, the days too humid, for it to be a paradise. For the energetic there are squash and tennis courts, and a nine-hole golf course which takes several hours and four salt tablets to go round, even in the cool of the late after-noon. The greens are known as browns.

Membership of the centre is a zealously guarded privilege, and only twenty-five non-employees of the oil company are allowed to join. The beach, though, is open to anyone. On the long swings provided for children, one can often see complete Omani families sitting, the women covered from head to foot in black, flowing robes, gently rocking backwards and forwards.

It is to Ras al Hamra that the oil men come on their days off. Fahud and the other oil camps are all for men only, and the families live at the coast. For every fourteen days a man spends in the Interior, he is given a week off. Apart from work there is little to occupy him at Fahud: the bar, the cinema, a swimming pool (rarely used until the sun has gone down), tennis courts with floodlights because it is too hot to play during daylight, squash courts and another small golf course. And walking. Not far from the camp is a valley full of the most beautiful fossils, a re-minder of the prehistoric days when Oman was the bed of the sea, and most oil men spend time collecting them.

The land on which the oil has been dis-covered belongs to the Duru, a Bedou tribe. The tribal make-up of Oman is complicated but important, because tribal loyalties have tradi-tionally been the vital ones. The tribes which have always held the power in Oman have been the settled tribes – the farmers – who built towns and fortified them. Less numerous, but occupying as much as 80 per cent of the land area, are the Bedou, the nomadic people who wander the deserts and semi-desert wastes on the fringes of the settled areas. They sleep out under the stars, with only the occasional tree as a roof, and as their herds of goats and sheep move slowly from one grazing area to the next, they follow with all their possessions. The urge to wander seems to be dying as more and more Bedou gravitate towards the towns, and it is probable that in a few generations most will have become settled. The tribes are run as loose-knit families, as

WATERMELON SELLERS, ROSTAQ SOUK

BUTCHER, ROSTAQ SOUK

THE SHEIKH'S MAJLIS, AL GHAFAT

FATHER AND SON, ROSTAQ SOUK

the Scottish clans must once have been, and there are more than two hundred of them, some with as few as one hundred members. Each has a head, a Sheikh and every major tribal grouping has also a Tamimah, a paramount Sheikh. The army officer accompanying us asked us what tribe we belonged to in London; he could not understand that we do not have such groupings in England.

The camels of the Duru wander freely through the oil camp at Fahud, foraging in the dustbins for food, eating anything they can find. Because of the company agreement with the tribe, PDO cannot fence off the compound, and although the camels are a nuisance, owners can never be found – until one is killed. Then an irate Bedou will materialize from nowhere and demand compensation. There is a set scale of payments for a dead camel: seventy rials (about $200 or £100) for a female (it might be more if she is pregnant) and fifty rials for a male. Since an owner will claim compensation however his beast has died, the onus to prove it was killed by an oil company vehicle or employee is always on him.

One of the men responsible for sorting out such claims is Khamis al Sharif, a senior Omani employee of PDO. It was principally to film him that we went to Fahud. He is an industrial-relations assistant and most of his work is concerned with recruiting labour. He has to negotiate with the Sheikhs of the area who supply the work-force. Each local tribe has an allocation of work, which formerly involved a complete change of work-force every month. They have managed to sort this out, so that they now have a continuity of labour, but the tribes still have their allocations, and Khamis's job is to go to the Sheikhs for additional labour or replacements.

His other main task is to deal with personnel problems, which he does in the time-honoured manner by getting the disputing parties together in his *majlis*, sitting on the floor and talking out an answer. While we were with him, there was a long and intensive dispute about whether a Bedford truck which took workers back to the village of Bahla should drive right through the village. One of the workers was complaining that he was dropped on the edge of the village and had to walk to the other side to reach his house. He could see no reason why the truck should not drop him at his door, which the driver refused to do. Khamis went with them both to Bahla and discovered that, although the Bedford could just squeeze through the narrow streets, it could not turn round at the other end and would have to back up a mile through the village in order to get out again. If, by chance, it should meet another vehicle there would be an inextricable traffic-jam. The chances were, too, that the truck would take half the walls of the houses with it if it did attempt the journey. Khamis decided the man must walk, and he was not pleased.

Khamis is a small, shy man in his forties, eloquent and charming. He talked about the days of Said bin Taimur without rancour or bitterness, finding it almost as unbelievable as we did that conditions could have been so bad. He was once in the old Sultan's army. When his British officer wanted to promote him, the Sultan himself said no, and the officer advised Khamis to resign. He went to Kuwait to work for an oil company, but missed Oman so much that he returned to join PDO in a lowly position two years before the coup. Although he was not personally involved in any form of rebellion against Said bin Taimur, he is quite definite that if open revolt had flared up he would have joined it.

He used to work in headquarters at Mina al Fahal, but hardly ever saw his family in the Interior, and so he now works at Fahud the whole time. Khamis's marriage was arranged for him by his parents, when he was in his teens and his wife was about ten. He doesn't know her exact age, only that it was four years after their wedding before she had her first period. He considers himself very fortunate to have been given a wife he has grown to love. He lives a traditional life at Yanqul, in the mountains north of Ibri, far removed from the European surroundings of Fahud. He took us home with him, but under no circumstances could we or he persuade his wife to be filmed. We did see her fleetingly in the background, preparing food, but she would not even meet us. She has even refused to have a photograph taken with her children for Khamis to keep at Fahud.

His mud and brick house is divided into quarters around a courtyard. If visitors call, men are received by the male members of the household, women by the females. The two never mix. Should they stay for a meal, the men sit at one end of the courtyard, the women and children at the other.

In the days before Qaboos, when vehicles were not allowed to drive from Muscat to Yanqul, a journey had to terminate at Ibri. If one of his children fell ill, Khamis could not take him to the American Mission hospital in Muscat, the only hospital in the country. If nature did not effect a cure, the child would just die. This was part of Said bin Taimur's policy: 'We don't need hospitals here,' he used to say. 'This is a poor country which can only support a small population. At present many children die in infancy and so the population doesn't increase. If we build clinics many more will survive – but for what? To starve?'

After the revolution, Khamis and a cousin financed a clinic at Ibri, paying for a doctor and a nurse to come from India. He still runs this venture and will continue until the new government hospitals and clinics can take over. Yanqul itself now has a hospital, a school and a clinic under construction, but Khamis quite expects it to take another ten years before his village is living a modern life. Although he welcomed the revolution and the changes it brought, he does not accept everything uncritically. Many aspects of development disturb him, as they do all the older traditionalist Omanis. He is a devout Moslem and gets very cross when it is suggested that Islam has been responsible for holding back development and progress. He disapproves strongly of alcohol and smoking, and is concerned at the possible effects of modernization on family life. He finds it hard to believe that families can live apart as they do in the West, and the idea of putting an aged parent into a home fills him with horror.

Khamis bridges the old world and the new. He is aware that his children will lead different lives from his own traditional one, and yet, above all, he does not want them to abandon the standards of Islam which he sees as the cornerstone of Omani society. It is the dilemma of any thinking man, anywhere in the world, who welcomes progress but fears the side-effects of change.

Musandum and Dhofar; Oman's Future

The Musandum peninsula is cut off from the rest of Oman by the eastern section of the United Arab Emirates. It is an area of bare rock rising sheer out of the sea to heights of over 5,000 feet. It has few inhabitants, some of whom still live in caves. It is said to be the hottest place in the world. From time to time throughout history the great powers have tried to establish bases on the peninsula. The most notable attempt was ordered by Lord Curzon, Viceroy of India, in 1901. He deemed Musandum to be a vital link in the defence of the British sphere of influence against the Russians. He decreed that three flagstaffs must be erected there; but they and the British presence have vanished without trace.

Today, 62 per cent of the West's oil passes through the channel no more than three miles wide that runs between the northern tip of the Musandum peninsula and a rock, also belonging to Oman, on which stands a lighthouse. Thus the lifeblood of Europe's industry passes through Omani territorial waters.

The Straits of Musandum were clearly a spectacular sight, and we asked to be flown there so that we could film them and the passing tankers. The flight in a light aircraft to the landing strip at Khasab, where the military garrison for the peninsula has its camp, takes about two hours. It was uneventful until almost the last few minutes. Then, flying up a creek which looked rather like a fjord, we spotted a shoal of about a hundred giant rays below us. From 2,000 feet they looked as if someone had scattered handfuls of postage stamps in the water. Circling lower to get a better look we saw that two were being devoured by sharks. The rays must have been all of thirty feet across. They sometimes leap completely clear of the water and fall backwards to dislodge parasites; if they do this close to fishermen they can completely swamp their boats.

Landing at Khasab moments later was a hair-raising business. Flying in low over the sea, we crossed a little town and headed for a sheer wall of rock. At the last moment the pilot flipped the little plane up, banked right, and we cleared the top of the rock and curled sideways down into a basin of mountains. In no time we were facing the way we had come and dropping on to a grey, stony landing strip marked by oil drums.

We were met at the plane and taken to the officers' mess. They seemed glad to have visitors; it is a lonely posting, and the officers' main recreation is fishing for sharks.

Next morning, we were flown by helicopter out into the straits to film the sunrise. The helicopter put three of us down on a bare cone-shaped rock about a mile from the headland. It then left us to go and get more fuel. As we stood with our camera, waiting for the sun, the engine of the helicopter died away to nothing. In the silence we realized that we were completely alone. It was then that we remembered that we had forgotten to unload any water. What if something went wrong and the helicopter didn't return? Once the sun came up there would not be a single foot of shade anywhere on the rock. We remembered the story of a British party, landed from a ship in the nineteenth century on one of the inlets at Musandum, who had been discovered three days later, dead from the heat.

Such thoughts were banished from our minds by the sun rising above the mountains of Iran. Minutes later our helicopter returned.

The pilot said he would take us to a spot where we would get a spectacular view. The altimeter was reading 3,000 feet and in a few moments we were hovering on the edge of a sheer cliff. Round and round he flew, checking where there might be gusts of wind and trying to find a level spot big enough for the helicopter's skids. Gingerly he let the machine down on a bare, smooth slab, an angry greenish dragonfly perched on a massive wall of rock. The tail of the helicopter jutted out over the cliff. As we opened the doors, he explained that he would have to leave the engine running so that he could make an immediate take-off if anything went wrong. We scrambled away, ducking under the blades. As we started to mount the camera a man appeared as if from nowhere. We assumed that he must be one of the troglodytes we had heard about, who are reputed to speak an unintelligible dialect. He came up and greeted us, shaking our hands with a friendly smile. What must he have thought of these strange men who appeared from a machine in the sky? The helicopter's engine roared, and we turned to see it banking sharply as it climbed into the sky. The rock on which it had been standing had started to crack under its weight.

While we had been filming the sunrise, a small Omani motor gunboat had sailed into view. Later we met her British commander, who told us he was on an official cruise up the Gulf, showing the Sultanate flag in the ports of the other Gulf states. He was a real marine explorer. There are few modern navigational charts for the coastal waters of Oman – most of those that do exist date back to the time of Nelson – and much of his time was spent exploring and mapping the coast.

We had heard that the Sultan plans to build up the strength of his navy, and the young officer said it would not be surprising, as the Omanis were very proud of their seafaring tradition and of the fact that the Oman was once the major sea power in the Indian Ocean. Back in Muscat we asked the Minister of Foreign Affairs if such unconfirmed stories were true. 'Yes,' he said, and went on, candidly and courteously, to explain why. First, Oman must have sufficient strength to police her own territorial waters against fishermen from the other Gulf states. Secondly, government policy was not to allow the right of 'free passage' through the Omani straits of Musandum, but to allow 'innocent passage'. Thus possession of the strategic straits of Musandum is vital to Oman's sovereignty.

Apart from Michael's visit to Salalah to meet the Sultan, none of us went south to Dhofar. We had originally intended to cover it, but we came to realize that it would have meant making a virtually separate film. Dhofar was not part of Oman at all until the nineteenth century, and the language and culture of its people are significantly different from the rest of the country. Dhofar occupies about 25 per cent of the land area of Oman. The part of the province bordering Saudi Arabia is barren desert and rock. The coastal strip catches the tip of the monsoon and so has sub-tropical vegetation, making it a valuable source of food. Immediately inland from the coast there is a high plateau, on which there is grassland where the tribesmen herd cattle. It is here that the insurgent activity has concentrated. Recently it has been increasingly contained; but, regrettably, it is still a sizeable drain on the nation's resources. Official figures state that 30 per cent of the national income is spent on defence, much of it on counter-insurgency.

Unfortunately for Oman, outsiders tend to think of the country as just another oil-rich Gulf state, which it most certainly is not. The annual income from oil is $600 million or £300 million a year – less than the annual trading loss of some of the nationalized industries in Great Britain – and this has to pay for everything: housing, hospitals, schools, roads, industry, mineral exploration, administration; all the projects that have been started since 1970. Furthermore, the experts consider that the commercial life of the known oil deposits is not likely to exceed another fifteen years. Additional finds have, it is true, recently been made in Dhofar, but so far they are of suspect quality and difficult to extract. The uses to which that limited income is now put will govern the future of Oman for many years to come.

In the space of five short years Oman has changed dramatically from a medieval society to a modern, developing nation. Progress at such a rate has meant vast expenditure on many and various projects, and the Omanis have on occasion been overcharged by unscrupulous foreign businessmen. With a backlog of centuries to clear almost overnight, virtually every project had a claim to priority; and the natural rivalries between regions, which Qaboos inherited, meant that if one major provincial town had a hospital, the next had to have one also. Everywhere schools were needed; there had to be roads and communications, including newspapers, telephones, radios and the infrastructure of an administration experienced enough to run the country.

Understandably, when enthusiasm and need went together with inexperience, spending quickly got out of hand, and by the end of the first five years Oman was temporarily in the red. For the moment, Qaboos has been forced to call a halt to new projects and has formed a Development Board to control and monitor all future spending. One of its most urgent tasks is to decide the priorities of the next five years, to weigh one development against another. Its policy document states that it should be borne in mind that oil is natural wealth and should benefit all society.

'Therefore it is not the right of the present generation to have it but the harvest must be for the benefit of the present and future generations. It is our responsibility to use these revenues in a way so that our development flourishes and our future is secured. The benefits should go to all areas of the Sultanate and our people. The people should have hope for a peaceful and better life. The main object of the development programme at this stage should be to put into action those projects which will become sources of revenue to stand side by side with the oil revenues, thus guaranteeing the financial future of the country.'

Industry was low on the list of priorities in 1970. But now a new start has already been made on some projects which it is hoped will stabilize the country's economy and move it away from total dependency upon oil. A cement works, a plant for the production of fertilizer and a flour-mill are now under construction. Little could be accomplished in the Interior during the first five years, for the simple reason that to build a factory in the Interior presents almost insurmountable problems: there are no roads to get equipment to the site, no accommodation for the work-force, no food, no electricity, no skills; every-thing from the cement to the labourers has to be imported.

In the search for alternative sources of income, natural resources play an important part. Centuries ago, copper was mined in the northern mountains, to which explorers are now looking for further mineral wealth. An American-Canadian consortium plans a copper-smelting works near Sohar; and manganese, asbestos and other important minerals have been discovered in the mountains north of Muscat. It remains to be seen whether they are in sufficient quantities to warrant commercial extraction.

One of the greatest of Oman's natural resources is the sea, which washes more than a thousand miles of her shores. It bubbles with edible fish: tuna, marlin, mackerel, parrot fish, sardine and shark – the last considered a great delicacy in Oman. The Government is planning to replace the traditional fishing fleets of canoes and dugouts with large modern trawlers which will be able to stay at sea for several days, backed up by deep-freeze facilities. Lobsters from Masirah, reputed to be the finest anywhere, could soon be gracing the gourmet tables of the world.

Oman is unique in Arabia for its immense potential for growing food. With well-planned husbandry, Oman could become largely self-sufficient for food as well as having a healthy surplus for export. Much work is being done to find out which fruits and crop strains are best adapted to the climate, and a multi-purpose cannery is being built on the Batinah Coast. The potential for stock-raising is under close scrutiny, especially in Dhofar, and it may be that Oman will become a small-scale meat exporter.

Many of the agricultural hopes depend on water. Apart from the monsoon regions of the south, rain provides neither a direct nor a reliable source of water; indeed, average rainfall figures over the years barely rise from the bottom of the graph. The main source of water is the ground; it is brought to the areas that need it either from a well or along the traditional *falaj*. A number of water surveys are being conducted, but these seem to indicate that all major water resources are being tapped. In such a situation, the new desalination plant on the coast assumes enormous importance.

The greatest single natural resource of Oman is her people: well-mannered, cultured, charming, unspoilt by the trappings of modern society. Everyone we met impressed us. To train them to run their own country will take an agonizing amount of time. When Qaboos took over, the literacy rate was 5 per cent, and almost all middle management and above had to be imported. Literacy is now increasing dramati-cally, but there are still 50,000 foreigners in the country (out of a total population of under three-quarters of a million), and Oman will be heavily dependent upon them for many years to come.

Another area where much still needs to be done is low-cost housing. Yet there is uncertainty over what form this should take. Understandably the modern Omani may not feel he is progressing unless he owns a Western-style, cement-block house, despite its need for air-conditioning which consumes energy and money that could perhaps be better spent elsewhere. But, equally, for many Omanis the *barasti* is part of a traditional life-style they do not wish to change. It is cool, keeps out the rain, is easy and cheap to maintain. Despite its primitive appearance, it is functional, and a simple concrete plinth on which to build a new one is all that many inhabitants would ask. Even on a grander scale, the traditional mud-and-brick houses are far more practical for the country's needs. On this, as on many points, the Omani people will have to try to find a compromise compounded of their traditions and their need for progress.

Modernization perforce brings greater wealth and mobility to the workers, involves them with the running of the country, and thus may weaken family ties. Young people move to the capital to find work, away from their mothers, brothers and sisters; and families, so important in Moslem society, are threatened. If Sultan Qaboos can succeed in maintaining the traditional standards of Islam which have controlled Omani society for more than 1,000 years, it will be a major achievement which will ensure the disciplined continuity of his reign.

But most of these problems are examples of the growing-pains which everywhere attend development on any significant scale: only, in Oman, the normal rate of progress has been so accelerated that her difficulties have been thrown into sharper relief. But this has its positive side, for often problems have not had time to become embedded in society, or to create their own areas of vested interest, before they are discovered and weeded out. With good will and enthusiasm, anything should be possible in Oman; it has wealth and the vigour which comes from a new ruler anxious to sweep away the darkness of the immediate past.

It is true that we came to Oman with some slight misgivings; but we left with a real regret.

The country has had its internal divisions, and the rawness and friction which comes of haste. But Sultan Qaboos has made extraordinary progress since he came to power. And each day that he rules, the cement that binds his nation together becomes firmer. Qaboos bin Said is called by some the 'Shepherd of Oman'. We left his land with a confident hope that he will be able to lead his people into united and prosperous pastures.